The Art of Drama, vol

Macbeth

PERIPETEIA PRESS

Published by Peripeteia Press Ltd.

First published September 2019

ISBN: 978-1-9997376-5-8

Check out our A-level English Literature website, peripeteia.webs.com

Contents

Introduction	5
Writing about plays	6
Stagecraft	11
Dialogue & conversation analysis	36
The nature of the play	38
The big themes	44
Shakespeare's language	60
The playwright	74
Shakespeare's world	77
Critical commentaries	81
Act One	81
Act Two	87
Act Three	96
Act Four	103
Act Five	109
The soliloquies	118
Critical essays on characters	124
Macbeth	125
Lady Macbeth	132
Banquo & Fleance	138
Macduff	146
The Witches	151
Other characters: Duncan, Malcolm et al	159
Critical reception	165
Teaching & revision	168
Glossary	175
Recommended reading	179

Introduction to *The Art of Drama* series

The philosopher Nietzsche described his work as 'the greatest gift that [mankind] has ever been given'. The Elizabethan poet Edmund Spenser hoped his book *The Faerie Queene* would magically transform readers into noblemen. In comparison, our aims for The Art of Drama series of books are a little more modest. Fundamentally we aim to provide books that will be of maximum use to students of English and to their teachers. In our experience, few GCSE students read essays on literary texts, yet, whatever specification they are studying, they have to produce their own analytical essays. So, we're offering some models, written in a lively and accessible style.

In this new series of books, we aim to reproduce the success of our *The Art of Poetry* series by providing fine-grained, well-informed and engaging material on the key issues in key GCSE set texts. In the first book in the series, we focused on J. B. Priestley's popular old stager, *An Inspector Calls.* In this, the second in our series, we turn our critical attention to Shakespeare's notoriously dark and troubling Scottish play.

As with our poetry books, we hope this new series will appeal to all teachers and students of Literature. However, there is a plethora of material already available on *Macbeth* on the market. Many books aimed at GCSE pupils present information in condensed, broken up or broken down and bullet pointed formats. Our critical guide is distinguished by a focus on complete essays and on our aim to stimulate students aiming for level 7 and above in their English Literature GCSE. This book is arranged into four parts: introductory material, critical appreciation of key scenes, exemplar essays and teaching & revision ideas. We hope you will find it interesting and useful.

Writing about plays

The play and the novel

Plays and novels have several significant features in common, such as characters, dialogue, plots and settings. In addition, pupils read plays in lessons, often sitting at desks in the same way as they read novels. So it's not surprising that many pupils treat these two related, but distinct, literary art forms as if they were indistinguishable. Time and again, teachers and examiners come across sentences such as 'In the novel Macbeth…' Though sometimes this can be just a slip of the pen, often this error is a good indicator of a weak response. Stronger responses fully appreciate the fact that *Macbeth* is a play, written for the stage, by a playwright and realise the implications of the writer's choice of the dramatic form.

Characterisation

Imagine you're a novelist writing a scene introducing a major character. Sit back and survey the rich variety of means at your disposal: You could begin with a quick pen portrait of their appearance, or you could have your characters say or do something significant. Alternatively, you could use your narrator to provide comments about, and background on, the character. Then again, you might take us into the character's thoughts and reveal what's really going on inside their head. If you're trying to convey thought as it happens you could use a stream of consciousness.

Now imagine that you're a playwright. Sit up and survey the far more limited means at your disposal. Though you could describe a character's appearance, you'd have to communicate this through stage directions, which, of course, a theatre audience would not be able to read or hear.

The same holds true for background information and narratorial style comments about the character. And unless you're going to use the dramatic devices known as the aside and the soliloquy, as famously Shakespeare did in his four great tragedies, you'll struggle to find a direct way to show what your character's really thinking. As a playwright, action and dialogue, however, are your meat and drink. For a novelist, being able to write dialogue is a useful skill; for a dramatist it's essential.

In general, drama focuses our attention on the outward behaviour of characters. Skilfully done, this can, of course, also reveal interior thoughts. Nevertheless, novels more easily give access to the workings of the mind. You may have noticed this when novels are adapted into films and directors have to make the decision about whether to use a voiceover to convey the narrator or characters' thoughts. Rarely does this work uncheesily well.

Settings

With a swish of his or her pen or fingers over a keyboard, a novelist can move quickly and painlessly from one setting to another. One chapter of a novel could be set in medieval York, the next on a distant planet in the distant future. The only limitation is the novelist's skill in rendering these worlds. What is true for geographical settings is also true for temporal ones. A novelist can write 'One hundred years later…' or track a character from cradle to grave or play around with narrative time, using flashbacks and flashforwards.

Though a little more restricted, a modern film director can also move fairly easily between geographical and temporal settings and can cross-cut between them. Not so a playwright. Why? Because plays are written for an actual physical stage and radically changing a stage set during the action of a play is a tricky and potentially cumbersome business. Imagine your Medieval York hamlet, with its ramshackle thatched huts, pig pens and dirty streets. How are you going to transform this set to the dizzyingly futuristic world of Planet Zog in 2088 A.D. and without your audience noticing?

Possibly you could get your stage technicians dismantle and construct the different stage sets while the audience waits patiently for the action to restart. But wouldn't that be clumsy, and rather break the spell you'd hope your play was weaving? More likely you'd use a break, perhaps between scenes or, better, during the interval for the major re-arrangement of stage scenery.

Practically speaking, how many different stage sets could you create for a single play? Minimalistic stage designs might allow you to employ more settings, but you'd still be far more restricted than a film director or a novelist. And then there's the cost. Theatres aren't usually flushed with money and elaborate stage sets are likely to be very expensive. Another way out of this would be to have a pretty much bare and unchanging stage set and convey changes in scenes through the dialogue, a technique we'll see Shakespeare employ:

Character 1: What is this strange, futuristic place?
Character 2: Why, this must be the capital city of the Planet Zog.

Etc.

Though, as we'll also see, Shakespeare tends to do this a little more subtly than we have.

Plays also tend to be written chronologically, i.e. with time always moving forward. Partly this is because as we watch plays in real time, it's difficult to convey to an audience that a particular scene is actually a flashback and is set in the past. There are exceptions, of course, to this chronological trend. Notably Harold Pinter's *Betrayal*, for instance, in which the action of the play unfolds backwards from the present to past.

The time frame of a play also tends to be limited – days, weeks, perhaps even months, but very rarely years, decades or centuries. After all, it's not easy for an actor, or series of actors, to convincingly present characters aging over a prolonged period.

The stage and the page

Physicists and chemists have many things in common, as do rugby and football players, and vets and doctors. Novelists and playwrights also have many things in common, but they work in distinctly different fields. You wouldn't want a chemist teaching you physics, ideally, or depend on a rugby player to score a crucial FA cup goal. Nor would you want a vet to operate on you if you were ill, or for your GP to treat your darling pet. And, with only a few exceptions, nor would you want to read a novel written by a playwright or witness a play written by a novelist. Precious few writers excel in both literary forms [Samuel Beckett, Chekhov and Michael Frayn come to mind, but few others] which underlines the point about the different demands of writing for the stage and for the page.

Novels take place in the theatre of the reader's mind; plays take place in an actual physical space, on an actual stage. For the latter to happen, a whole load of people other than the writer have to be involved – directors, actors, designers, producers, technicians and so forth. And this takes us to the heart of another crucial difference between reading a play, reading a novel and seeing a play on a stage.

In a novel, the novelist can fill in the details of what is happening around the dialogue, such as gestures made by the characters:

'Did they even have pig-pens in medieval York?' asked Mikey, cocking his left eyebrow in a typically aggressively quizzical manner.

Neil thought for a moment, and then shrugged. 'Possibly not, but that's not really the point,' he said hopefully.

When we **read** a play, sometimes these details are apparent from stage directions. However, in a play we cannot see what characters are doing while other characters are speaking and we all too easily we can forget that silent characters are even present in a scene. When we **watch** a play, however, actors reveal how their characters are reacting to what other characters are saying, and often these reactions convey crucial information about relationships, feelings and atmosphere. We know, for instance, how Macbeth reacts to Duncan's announcement of his son, Malcolm's, succession to the throne, but what about Banquo? How does he feel about this news? Is all his attention on his King, or, remembering the Witches' prophecy, does he notice the impact of the King's words on his friend? These are crucial things for actors and directors to decide. Without this visual dimension, it is all too easily for readers to ignore the things that are supposed to be happening in the narrative background while each character is speaking. If a play on a page is similar to a musical score awaiting performance, a play on the stage is like the concert itself.

Focusing on the dramatic devices used by a playwright has a double benefit: Firstly, all good analytical literary essays concentrate on the writer's craft; secondly, such a focus emphasises to the examiner that you understand the nature of the type of text you're exploring, a play, and distinguishes you from many other readers who don't really appreciate this fact. In the next section we'll sharpen our focus on the playwright's craft by honing in on stagecraft.

Stagecraft

When you're writing about a novel it's always productive to focus on narration. Narration includes narrative perspective, such as first and third person, types of narrator, such as naïve and unreliable, as well as narrative techniques, such as the use of dialogue, cross-cuts and flashbacks. Narration is worth focusing your attention on because it's an absolutely integral feature of all novels and short stories. In plays the equivalent of narration is called stagecraft. Examining stagecraft is an incisive and revealing way to spot the writer at work. Some playwrights are able to use all the craft and resources of the theatre, namely set, props, costumes, lighting and music, while for various reasons [technical, artistic, budgetary] other playwrights may be more restricted.

Shakespeare, for instance, doesn't really use lighting in his plays, except notably in *The Winter's Tale*, because most of his plays were performed at the Globe theatre and in daylight. His instructions on costume are also very limited, usually embedded within the texts, rather than stated separately in stage directions. Think, for example, of Malvolio's yellow cross-gartered stockings in *Twelfth Night* or Hamlet's inky suit of woe. On the other hand, the importance of costumes is underlined repeatedly in Shakespeare's plays by characters who disguise themselves by changing their clothes. For instance, Viola becoming Cesario in *Twelfth Night* or Kent and Edmund disguising themselves in *King Lear*. Repeatedly too, villainy in Shakespeare's plays tries to remain hidden under a layer of fine clothes. Think, for instance, of Lady Macbeth's injunction to her husband in Act I Scene 5 to look 'like the innocent flower/ But be the serpent under't'.

The general sparsity of information about costumes has, however, allowed directors over the years to relocate Shakespeare's plays to all sorts of settings with a huge variety of matching costumes. In a recent RSC production of *Antony and Cleopatra*, for instance, the designs for the Egyptian queen's costumes were inspired by powerful contemporary female celebrities such as Beyoncé.

When a playwright is restricted in the range of stagecraft he or she can utilise, not only do the devices they employ become more prominent, but other integral aspects of stage business also become more significant. In *Macbeth*, as in *An Inspector Calls*, for instance, exits and entrances are particularly important. Indeed, the managing of exits and entrances is at the core of all plays. Exits facilitate changes in costume and allow actors to recover from or prepare for major scenes. Tracking these seemingly simple instructions always uncovers interesting and significant patterns, particularly in terms of which characters know what information at crucial points in the action.

Stage sets

As we mentioned in our discussion of the key differences between novels and plays, the latter invariably have fewer settings due to the fact that dramatic texts have to be physically realised in stage designs. And, as we also noted, changing from one elaborate stage set to another presents problems for directors and, potentially for the finances of a production. What sort of choices does a stage designer have to make when creating a set? Firstly, a lot depends on the nature of the play, as well as the playwright, the director and the budget. Some playwrights are very particular about the settings of their plays and describe them in tremendous detail.

The American playwright Tennessee Williams, for instance, wrote particularly poetic stage directions, such as those that open his play *A Streetcar Named Desire*: 'First dark of an evening in May' and the 'sky is a peculiarly tender blue, almost turquoise, which invests the scene with a kind of lyricism and gracefully attenuates the atmosphere of decay'. If that isn't enough to get a stage designer shake and scratch their head, Williams finishes with a synesthetic poetic flourish 'you can almost feel the warm breath of the brown river' that is even more challenging to realise on stage.

Other playwrights will sketch out far more minimalistic sets. Samuel Beckett in *Waiting for Godot*, for instance, describes the stage set in the sparest way possible, using just six simple words: 'A country road. A tree. Evening'.

[Despite the skeletal detail, in production, Beckett was notoriously specific and exacting about how he wanted the stage to be arranged.]

Even if the playwright doesn't provide a great deal of information about the exact setting, a director is likely to have an overall concept for a play and insist, albeit to varying degrees, that the set design fit with this. If, for instance, a director wishes to bring out the contemporary political resonances of a play such as *Julius Caesar* she or he might dress the characters like well-known American politicians and set the play in a place looking a little like the modern White House. Similarly, Shakespeare's *Richard III* has often been relocated to an imagined modern fascistic state.

Given free reign, a stage designer has to decide how realistic, fantastical, symbolic and/or expressionist their stage set will be. The attempt to represent what looks like the real world on stage, as if the audience are looking in through an invisible fourth wall, is called verisimilitude and is the equivalent of photographic realism in fine art.

Stage sets for *Macbeth*

What are the various spaces that directors and stage designers have to imagine for *Macbeth*? The stage direction for the opening scene simply says 'an open space'. This may or may not be the same space where we find the Witches again in scene three when they are on a 'heath'. Other scenes in Act I take place at a 'camp near Florres', in a 'room in the King's palace' at Florres, then a 'room in Macbeth's castle' in Inverness, as well as outside the same castle. Finally we end up in scene seven within the castle again, again in a presumably different, but also non-specified room. That's an awful lot of chopping and changing in a short space of time. And, indeed, although *Macbeth* is one of Shakespeare's shorter plays it contains twenty-nine scenes - nine more than *Hamlet* - so its scenes tend to be short and the pace of the play fast. Of course, Shakespeare was writing for the Globe stage, as shown below, and, as we have already mentioned, his plays were always performed during daylight hours. So, stage scenery signalling all these different locations would have been very minimal. The three levels of the Globe stage - beneath, on, and above the main stage - were associated with hell, earth and heaven, so it may be the Witches entered from the trap-door below the stage to signal their demonic nature. [Indeed, Shakespeare explicitly uses the trap-door in this symbolic way later in the play, in Act IV Scene 1, when the various 'apparitions' that visit Macbeth at the Witches' bidding are given the stage direction to 'descend' after their appearance]. Whichever way they enter and exit, and whatever small bits of stage set might suggest a 'heath', the Witches' costumes, the accompanying 'thunder' and their witchy, incantatory dialogue would have to have evoked most of the atmospheric scene setting.

Even for a modern production, the quick shifting in Act I between up to six different places would also make it impractical to devise elaborately different stage designs for each scene. In well-resourced productions a rotating stage might be used to facilitate smooth transitions between places. Probably a modern director and their stage designer would be keen to emphasise the contrast between the wild, ungoverned exterior spaces of scenes one and three and the seemingly more ordered and civilised interior spaces of the two castles at Florres and Inverness. How might we distinguish between Duncan's castle and the Macbeth's Dunsinane?

Noticeably the scenes in Florres take place in daylight and the King's entrance to his castle is signalled by a bright 'flourish of trumpets'. In contrast, by the time the royal party have arrived at Inverness night is already falling, as indicated by the carrying of carrying of 'torches'. The same props are used again at the start of scene seven and are also carried in Act II, even though the second act is set during day time. Indeed, in scene four Ross tells the old man explicitly that, despite the coming of morning, 'darkness does the face of the earth entomb' at Macbeth's castle. Trumpets are also replaced by 'hautboys' and these medieval oboes go on to feature again later in the play. As the Shakespeare Birthplace Trust makes clear the harsh sounds of this instrument were often used by Shakespeare to generate an ominous atmosphere presaging doom[1]. A modern director can, of course, employ lighting to really emphasise the distinctly darker, constantly darkening and foreboding atmosphere of the Macbeths' castle.

The rest of the play's action takes place in a number of other settings: In Act III Scene 3, Banquo is murdered in another external space, a 'park, with a road leading to the palace'. Once again murderous acts occur in gloomy, dying light. The first murderer tells us that there are a few 'streaks of day' left in the sky, Banquo informs us that the night is pitch-black and both Banquo and one of the murderers call out for a 'light'. If audiences hadn't already appreciated the symbolic darkness Shakespeare has one of the hired killers shout 'Who did strike out the light' immediate after Banquo's murder.

Act III Scene 4 takes place within Macbeth's castle again, but this time in a room big enough to host a 'banquet'. Whereas it's difficult to distinguish such spaces on the Globe stage, a modern director in a modern theatre would probably wish to establish a strong contrast between the intimate, private spaces of Dunsinane, where Lady Macbeth and her husband can express their secret fears and darkest desires, and the public space of the banqueting room where they have to put on their masks and act their parts in the social intercourse.

---

[1] https://www.shakespeare.org.uk/explore-shakespeare/blogs/ominous-oboes/

Act III Scene 5 takes place back on the heath, but by Act IV Scene I the Witches have relocated within a 'dark cave', with a 'boiling cauldron' in its middle. We can only speculate about how Shakespeare would have been able to create this dark cave, but it'd be easy enough on a modern stage with modern lighting. Rather loosely, Scene 6 is set, 'somewhere in Scotland', which leaves plenty of room for the director's imagination. The point, it seems, is that the scene could take place anywhere in Scotland because it's expressing sentiments about Macbeth's rule that could be found everywhere in Scotland.

During Act IV, two new places are added, the castles of Macduff, in Fife, and of Edward the Confessor, the English King, somewhere in England. The former will host another murder and the latter is where Duncan's son, Malcolm finds refuge. Of these two settings, Edward's castle is the more significant. A few well-placed flags might be enough to establish the Englishness of Edward's court. On the other hand, the graceful and 'most pious' English king is presented as an opposite to Macbeth who, by this point, has become a hated and bloody tyrant. If Dunsinane is characterized by its dark and gloomy interiors, potentially even becoming the physical embodiment of the Macbeths' murderous and guilt-ridden minds, Edward's castle might be defined by healing and cleansing light.[2]

In Act V, the action in multiple scenes flips back and forth between the 'country near Dunsinane' and in various parts of a 'field' or 'plain' outside the castle. Again, an antithesis appears to have been set up and then destabilized, between safe interior, supposedly civilized spaces and wild, exterior, dangerous exteriors. After Macbeth has been vanquished, the victors enter his castle with a bold trumpet 'flourish'. There are a further two trumpet flourishes, including one after the play's closing lines. There's no reference to 'torches' or to those ominous hautboys. Hence Dunsinane castle and by implication all the other Scottish castles has been re-captured, cleansed and restored to its proper function as a place of hospitality, civilisation and security.

_____

[2] With these staging ideas in mind it would be interesting to compare several film and/or theatre productions of *Macbeth*.

Other stage directions

Most playwrights include stage directions within their scripts. By convention written in italics and/or brackets, these directions often establish the setting of a scene, outline lighting or music, suggest costume, convey physical action and sometimes also indicate to the actors how lines should be spoken. In *Who's Afraid of Virginia Woolf*, for example, the playwright, Edward Albee provides lots of extra information alongside the actual words his characters say. Here's a short extract that illustrates the point [in the extract a married woman, Martha, is flirting outrageously with a younger married man, Nick, in front of both his wife, Honey and Martha's own husband, George]:

MARTHA   [*to George...still staring at Nick, though*]: SHUT UP! [*Now, back to Nick*] Well, have you? Have you kept your body?

NICK   [*unselfconscious... almost encouraging her*]: It's still pretty good. I work out.

MARTHA   [*with a half-smile*]: Do you!

NICK   Yeah.

HONEY   Oh, yes...he has a very...firm body.

MARTHA   [*still with that smile... a private communication with Nick*] Have you! Oh, I think that's very nice.

Through the stage directions, Albee indicates to the actors where characters are looking, who they are at addressing at different moments, the tone they should adopt and even the facial expression the actors should put on. In addition, he uses capital letters as well as punctuation to convey tone and volume.

In contrast, Shakespeare's stage directions are minimalistic. As we've noted, at the start of scenes he establishes the setting with a just a few bold strokes of his quill. Take the opening scene's stage directions: '*A heath. Thunder. Enter Three Witches.*' Occasionally he does indicate when a character is addressing a particular person, or if there's an aside, and modern editors usually signal this with italicized comments in brackets, but in *Macbeth* Shakespeare never includes instructions at the starts of lines or, indeed anywhere else, about what tone the actor should express. Nor does he use capital letters and almost all of the punctuation we see in our scripts has been supplied by modern editors.

There are also very few stage directions that indicate stage action in *Macbeth*. Notably, when they do come, mostly they appear towards the end of the play when the fighting starts. Even at the climax of the play, Shakespeare leaves a lot of room for directors and actors to flesh out the action in a scene: '*Exeunt, fighting. Alarms. Re-enter fighting and Macbeth is slain*'. On the page, that can read rather dully, but done well on stage, a sword fight can be electrifying.

Nevertheless, there are subtler examples of stage directions in Shakespeare's plays, ones that are embedded within the action. A few examples will illustrate the point. Often these directions suggest how the actors should play a particular moment, as in Banquo's comment in Act I Scene 3, after the Witches have spoken to Macbeth, that his friend is 'rapt'; a clear behavioural prompt for the actor playing Macbeth. Similarly Lady Macbeth's comment to her husband that his face is a 'book where men/ may read strange matters' indicates to the actor he must look troubled. Again, later at the banquet, Lady Macbeth's line 'Shame itself! Why do you make such faces?', describing Macbeth's reaction to Banquo's ghost, is an embedded stage direction to the actor playing Macbeth.

At other times, rather than being separated out and put in brackets, stage action is indicated through dialogue. For example, when Banquo says to Fleance 'hold, take my sword' it clearly signals the physical exchange of the prop. During the banquet scene in Act III, Ross commands the assembled Lords to 'rise' from the table and is countermanded moments later by Lady Macbeth's instruction to 'Sit, worthy friends'. Sometimes there are also lines which suggest staging ideas: Banquo's comment that 'There's husbandry in heaven,/ Their candles are all out' could be interpreted as an embedded stage direction, telling the director that at this point the stage should be utterly dark. Check the text and you'll find many more similar examples.

More subtly, in Act I Scene 7, Shakespeare's distribution of the verse lines signals to the actors how to play this febrile conspiratorial scene. In almost every exchange in the scene the Macbeth's share one half of a line of verse each. This is most startlingly and snappily so when Macbeth most fears failure:

LADY MACBETH   …And dashed the brains out, had I so sworn as you
                    Have done to this.
MACBETH   If we should fail, -
LADY MACBETH   We fail?

A similarly rapid, percussive back-and-forth interaction occurs once Macbeth returns after committing the murder:

LADY MACBETH   Did you not speak?
MACBETH   When?
LADY MACBETH   Now.
MACBETH   As I descended?
LADY MACBETH   Ay.

The very short lines and their arrangement - in a pattern known as stichomythia - helps generate a sense of alarm and urgency.

A critic once commented that, unlike a modern film or even theatre director, Shakespeare didn't have any spectacular special effects at his disposal. But rather than detracting from his plays, this limitation is partly responsible for what makes them so extraordinary. Because for Shakespeare his language has to achieve these special effects.

Often, in addition to conveying the atmosphere to a director, the way Shakespeare has crafted his language indicates to an actor how to play a line or even a speech. Take, for instance, Macbeth's description of himself as he moves through his castle on his way to murder Duncan in Act II Scene 1:

'… Now o'er the one half world
Nature seems dead, and wicked dreams abuse
The curtained sleep; witchcraft celebrates

Pale Hecate's offering; and withered Murder…
… thus with his stealthy pace,
With Tarquin's ravishing strides, towards his design
Moves like a ghost – Thou sure and firm-set earth
Hear not my steps..'

We'll analyse this soliloquy in more detail later, but for now we'll just point out a few features that indicate how the scene should be played. Firstly, Shakespeare evokes an ominous atmosphere of evil, evil that is unloosed and at large, abusing the innocent. Secondly, the phrasing conveys Macbeth's feverishly conflicted, almost hallucinatory state of mind. On the one hand, he personifies himself as the capitalized 'Murder'. But on the other he qualifies this powerful figure with an adjective that implies age and weakness, and that also creates an echo, picked up by astute readers, of Banquo's description of the Witches. At the same time, he imagines himself to be like the Roman rapist Tarquin. The actor is also told how he should move, at a 'stealthy pace' and 'like a ghost', i.e. slowly and quietly. But even this is conflicted by those more eager 'ravishing strides'. And behaving stealthily, clearly the actor should be speaking his lines with hushed voice, making sure his feet make as little noise as possible across an otherwise entirely silent and utterly still stage.

Entrances and exits

Obviously in a play that has twenty-nine scenes there are a lot of entrances and exits and we've no intention of going through all of these now. However, paying close attention to who is and who isn't present in a scene, who comes in and who goes out, is always rewarding. Sometimes, indeed, the significance of a character's silent presence can be made more explicit on a stage than it might appear on the page and a character's absence from a scene may also be important. For practical reasons we'll limit this discussion to a handful of particularly significant examples.

Macbeth's entrance into Act I Scene 3, for instance, is significant as, though we have already heard a great deal about him as a character, this is the first time we actually see him in the flesh. Moreover, his entrance is critical because it suggests that the Witches may be exerting some sort of malign power and control over the world of the play. In the first scene they had predicted meeting with Macbeth 'ere the setting of sun' and when they hear a 'drum' they appear to know that it is Macbeth, and not some other general, who 'doth come'. You might object that this evidence doesn't really prove that the Witches shape events – perhaps they can only predict what will happen, but then Macbeth's first words of the play uncannily echo the Witches' own: 'So foul and fair a day'. [We'll consider the extent of the Witches' influence over the play in our essay on them later in this guide.]

In Act I Scene 6, the royal party arrive at Dunsinane and the stage directions at the start of the scene inform us that they enter, as would be expected, in hierarchal order, Duncan first, attendants last. It is noticeable that they are greeted by Lady Macbeth. This begs the question where is the king's host, her husband? Despite Lady Macbeth's dexterous finessing of the situation, Macbeth's absence is noted by Duncan: 'Where's the Thane of Cawdor?' Fortunately for the Macbeths, the king doesn't press the question harder and hence Lady Macbeth doesn't have to answer it, instead steering the conversation on to the safer ground of the servants. The notion that Macbeth might be guiltily avoiding Duncan is confirmed in the next scene where we find Macbeth alone, lost in his thoughts, introspectively mulling over his options. He is upbraided for not properly carrying out his duties as host by his wife because she understands the significance of his absence: 'He has almost supped. Why have you left the chamber?'

Having convinced her husband to commit regicide, Lady Macbeth ably supports him throughout the first half of the play. In Act II Scene 3, in quick succession, there are multiple entrances and exits and re-entrances during the discovery of Duncan's murder. A dangerous sense of disorder is generated by all this swift stage action: Within just seventy-odd lines Macduff and Lennox enter - Macbeth arrives - Macduff exits and then re-enters - Macbeth and Lennox 'exeunt' [i.e. leave together] - Lady Macbeth enters - Banquo joins the scene - Macbeth and Lennox re-enter - Malcolm and Donalbain enter and everyone exeunts, apart from Duncan's sons.

The critical moment in the scene, at least from the Macbeths' point of view, arrives when Macbeth has to explain why he left the room earlier and what he did while he was 'off-stage', visiting Duncan's chamber: 'O! yet I do repent of my fury/ That I did kill them.' He might have hoped in the general melee that this action would have been excused as hot-headed justice. But then Macduff asks a very dangerous, seemingly sceptical question:

'Wherefore did you so?'

Notice how these blunt and direct words complete a full line, suggesting that Macduff fires off his question immediately after Macbeth has spoken. Indicating a potential power shift in the scene, this question is, in effect, an imperative, ordering Macbeth to justify his actions. Something he then obviously struggles to do in the following ten stumbling lines. The sense that Macbeth is struggling to fully convince the gathered thanes could, of course, be brought out more on a stage, where the body language of Macduff and of the silent Banquo could be especially revealing. While we're thinking of silent presences, we might also note how Lennox says nothing[3]. Hadn't he visited

---

[3] In the revision activities we recommend tracking Lennox through the play's action. He's with Macbeth, for instance, when Macbeth visits the Witches, despite telling the Lord in the previous scene that Scotland is suffering under a 'hand accursed'.

Duncan's chamber with Macbeth as they exited the scene earlier together? In which case he must have witnessed Macbeth's actions. And yet he keeps his counsel at this crucial moment. If you were the actor playing Lennox what would you imagine going through his mind? How might you convey this on stage?

Sensing it seems Macbeth is floundering under the pressure, Lady Macbeth acts. A woman who has called on evil spirits to rid her of all pity is unlikely to be overwhelmed by the details of Duncan's murder, especially as she had a major hand in planning it. We're safe to assume, therefore, that her fainting is a pretence, designed to distract attention from the question her husband is failing to answer adequately. And her quick-thinking works too, to some extent. Attention is drawn away from Macbeth and he escapes the scene without having to give further account of killing the guards. On the other hand, neither Malcolm or Donalbain seem convinced that all is well, and Banquo's powerful speech reveals what he has been thinking during the previous interchanges.

Lady Macbeth's ingenuity will be tested again, this time to breaking point, during the banquet scene, Act III Scene 4. This scene starts, as the Macbeths would hope, with good order and a sense of unity. Stage directions inform us that the characters enter in the correct hierarchical order – Macbeth first, unnamed Lords and attendants last. Macbeth himself further emphasizes the importance of these protocols: 'You know your own degrees, sit down'. Ostensibly the Macbeths manage to maintain the pretence that all is well and in good order at the royal court despite the entrance of the disorderly figure of the first murderer at the doorway. Having ceded the bulk of the hosting responsibilities to his wife, Macbeth seems to juggle with his two audiences successfully enough. In one short passage, lines 9-12, he speaks in quick turns privately to his wife, to the whole company and then, presumably quietly, to the murderer. How successfully he carries this off will, of course, depend on how the scene is staged. Perhaps as they are being entertained a few of the Lords, maybe Lennox, might glance towards the doorway and wonder about the strange figure hovering at the edge of the feast. After all, Macbeth conducts a prolonged conversation with the murderer while no-one else it seems is speaking. Lady Macbeth, it appears, senses this, reminding her husband to turn his focus back on his guests: 'My royal lord/ You do not give the cheer…'

Her attempts to smooth things over, however, are about to be confounded by the entrance of Banquo's ghost. As many readers have noticed, the ghost arrives at precisely the moment Macbeth hypocritically mentions Banquo's absence. The disruption is not, however, immediate, as it appears the other characters are unable to see the ghost[4] and Macbeth himself doesn't recognise it as supernatural or as Banquo at first. A few lines later, however, now watched by his alarmed guests, Macbeth is addressing something invisible in the air: 'Thou canst not say I did it'. Up steps Lady Macbeth and into the breach. But, in spite of her attempts to scold and shame her husband, he is now lost to the horror before him. Out it all spills, until Lady Macbeth again tries to upbraid him, 'My worthy lord/ Your noble friends lack you'. For a moment Macbeth regains his composure and manages to address the company in what he hopes might be a jovial and convivial tone. But when he again mentions Banquo the ghost returns and Macbeth is cast back into the nightmare his actions have created, crying out, 'Hence horrible shadow!'

Still, ever more frantically, Lady Macbeth continues to try to distract from, cover up, excuse and explain her husband's wild and erratic behaviour, while simultaneously, and equally desperately, attempting to cajole him back into his senses. And despite all her best efforts, Macbeth is so lost that Ross's sudden question to him is a potential dagger thrust to the heart of his kingship:

'What sights, my lord?'

Imagine a sudden hush falling. Macbeth turning around to stare at Ross, perhaps even his mouth opening to speak. For a final time, Lady Macbeth

---

[4] Every director has to decide how to present Banquo's ghost. Would you choose the actor playing Banquo covered in gore and blood, or perhaps have nothing there but a sound effect? What differences might these choices make?

intervenes. Preventing her husband from having to answer such a perilous question, she takes a new tack, pleading with the assembled lords, 'I pray you speak not, he grows worse and worse'. Despite the Macbeths' attempts to orchestrate this banquet, to make it a powerful piece of political propaganda conveying order and unity it ends in utter shambles and division, protocol and decorum thrown wildly out of the window. The nobles might have entered the scene in orderly fashion, but their exit is chaotic: 'Stand not upon the order of your going/ But go at once'.

Duncan arrives at Dunsinane, from a 1936 production with interesting and surprising costume and set designs.

Props

Props can, of course, be used in all manner of ways. At the climax of Arthur Miller's *The Crucible*, the protagonist, John Proctor, signs a false confession of having committed witchcraft on a piece of paper. But when he is asked to give up this parchment by the court officials he will not, and his final defiance  is shown dramatically when he tears this prop in half. In Shakespeare's tragedy *King Lear*, the physical ring of the crown is an emblem of the impossibility of splitting the kingdom successfully between Lear's daughters and therefore of the foolishness of the king's plan. In many of Shakespeare's plays props in the form of physical letters are intercepted and fall dangerously into the wrong hands, moving on the plot.

Props can also be used as signals of character - heroes in Shakespeare's plays invariably brandish swords, while fops carry nosegays. Machiavellian villains always have a bottle of poison handy or wield poison pens, while cut-throat villains use daggers. Props can be used to heighten a dramatic effect and, as in the example from The Crucible to tell in a single image or action something it would take words longer to do.

Before you read the next section list any props you can remember appearing in the play. Try to arrange them in chronological order. Then write next to each one how they are used by the dramatist.

- Macbeth's letter

Generally it seems that this particular prop, the letter, is associated in Shakespeare's tragedies with villains and with conspiracies. In King Lear, the Machiavellian Edmund forges a letter in his innocent brother, Edgar's, hand to frame him in a plot to kill their father. Later in the same play another villainous character, one of Lear's daughters, Goneril sends instructions in a letter, a letter that, intercepted, becomes crucial evidence against her. In Hamlet, another Machiavellian villain, king Claudius, sends a letter to England instructing the immediate execution of his own nephew/step-son, Hamlet. Only this letter is intercepted by Hamlet and, re-written by him, leads to the execution of Claudius' stooges Rosencrantz and Guildenstern.

So letters in Shakespeare's tragedies are dangerous; associated with private secrets, with things that cannot be said in public, they often reveal cunning machinations and treacherous double-dealing. Falling into the wrong hands, they can rebound violently upon their writers. Macbeth writing a letter to his wife therefore links him not to other tragic heroes, but to Machiavellian villains, right from the start of the play. The letter confirms Macbeth continues to have 'black' and secret thoughts he cannot share with anyone else other than his 'dearest partner in greatness'. After the announcement of Malcolm's succession Macbeth could possibly have harboured his 'black and deep desires' but kept them to himself and suppressed them. Committing these thoughts to paper and sharing them with his wife marks the first definite step towards putting them into action.

- Torches
- Hautboys

We've already discussed how these two props / instruments are used to signal darkness and evoke a sinister atmosphere.

- Cups and dishes
- A banqueting table and chairs

As well as signalling the Macbeths' wealth and power, these props and/or pieces of stage scenery can be employed to emphasise the dramatic shift from order to disorder in Act III Scene 4. As the dialogue makes clear, everyone has a correct place at the table at the start of the scene, with a particular place set aside for Macbeth. The arrangement of the props might further stress this orderliness. As host, it is also Macbeth's role to lead the celebrations, to 'give the cheer' and propose the toasts, a role Lady Macbeth has to prompt him into remembering. The wine cups are essential props here. Presumably when Macbeth belatedly invites the lords to drink and they respond in unison with 'Our duties, and the pledge' they stand and drink from the cups. What do they do next, however, when as they are still rising from their seats or in mid-gulp Macbeth cries out 'Avaunt! And quit my sight!'? Certainly, Lady Macbeth's following comments imply that Macbeth's disorder has unsettled the whole banquet: 'you have displaced the mirth, broke the good meeting/ With most admired disorder'.

- Various swords and daggers

The function of these props as signals for a martial society is self-explanatory, we hope. Perhaps there is, however, a subtle distinction between the two: swords seem to be used exclusively for honourable battle, whereas daggers are associated with dirty deeds. At the start of the play Macbeth is reported to have defeated the Norwegian invaders with his 'brandished steel'; Banquo passes his 'sword' to Fleance in Act II Scene 1, and both Young Siward and Macduff fight Macbeth with swords at the end of the play. In contrast, Macbeth sees a 'dagger' floating in the air ahead of him when he goes to kill Duncan and uses daggers to do the deed. When his wife commands him to 'give me the daggers' she uses them to frame the guards. Shortly afterwards Malcolm comments shrewdly that 'there's daggers in men's smiles' and the murderers who kill Banquo and the Macduffs carry daggers.

Which characters are and which are not armed may also be significant. Certainly, the warriors – Macbeth, Banquo, Macduff, Young Siward and other lords, such as Lennox and Ross – must be armed in many if not every scene. But what about Duncan and his son Malcolm? There doesn't appear to be any reference in the play to either of these gentler characters specifically having a sword, though surely we'd expect the latter to be armed when his armies attack Dunsinane. A stage production might take up these textual hints, so that the elderly Duncan's lack of this prop is used to further emphasize both his vulnerability and dependency on others for his protection. If Malcolm does not carry a sword, then he is like his father, also dependent on warriors, in his case, Young Siward and Macduff.

- A pitcher of water

When he returns to their private chamber after committing regicide, Macbeth is literally obsessed with the blood on his hands: 'Ha! they pluck out my eyes/ What hands are here?' He imagines that all the water in the oceans would be needed to clean the guilt from these hands, and even then that would not be enough; he has so much blood on his hands that it would turn all the 'multitudinous seas' red. In contrast, Lady Macbeth conceives of the blood only in literal and pragmatic terms: 'A little water clears of this deed'. Though, there isn't a stage direction or mention of a prop in the text, in the manner of an embedded stage direction, like the ones we discussed earlier, the action suggests one.

A director who wants to underscore the link between this scene and Lady Macbeth's nightmarish sleepwalking in Act V Scene 1, could use the same prop. Though, once again, there is no mention of a prop in text, Lady Macbeth is clearly trying to clean the 'damned spot' from her hands, rubbing them together as if under water. On the other hand, doing this action without water would enhance the scene's hallucinatory quality, linking wife to husband.

- Lady Macbeth's taper

Lady Macbeth does, however, definitely carry a taper, which is a small, slender candle. The visual power of this inconstant, flickering and fragile symbol light can be emphasized in modern productions by darkening the stage at this

point. Such lighting would liberalise the darkness within which Lady Macbeth is trapped. In daylight, on the Globe stage, in contrast, Lady Macbeth's darkness is more psychological, more obviously a product of her own tortured mind. As a small point light in the encompassing darkness, the candle also, of course, is a symbol for Lady Macbeth's soul. Hence, in many productions the scene ends with her snuffing out the candle.

- Colours

In Act V Scene 2, the invading army enter with 'drums and colours'. We'll mention drums in the next section, but colours are flags carried by soldiers into battle to signal rallying points. The various flags on display could symbolize the unified forces of various disparate groups in opposition to the solitary and isolated Macbeth.

- Macbeth's head.

At the end of the play Macduff enters with Macbeth's head. Take a tour round The Globe or the RSC props department and you'll find plenty of severed heads, some more realistic than others. The point is that the play starts and ends with gruesome brutality. And perhaps, despite presenting himself as a more progressive king, Malcolm's victory is not going to usher in a new, more civilised age. Perhaps we are merely seeing the cycle of history turn. Just as Duncan relied on powerful warriors to protect himself and his nation, warriors who could revel in fearsome, bloody violence, so too his son's reign begins with Macduff's savage violence, while Malcolm stands by and applauds from the side lines.

Costumes

Fashion changes all the time and those of you with a keen eye for fashion will be able to spot what is in fashion and what's not each season. Different social

 groups also have associated fashions and these associations change over time. Think of the 'Doc' Marten boot, for instance, or pairs of Nike Air trainers. Costumes also suggest the age of characters and their social background. Think of a tweed jacket, for instance, or a pair of ripped dungarees. In Shakespeare's time the sumptuary laws were still in place. These laws dictated what people could and could not wear depending on their status in society. Fundamentally the higher your status the greater the range of clothes and material you were allowed to wear.

Naturally, some playwrights are very specific about costumes, while others are happy for directors, actors and designers to make their own choices. In some of Shakespeare's plays he does specify how particular characters should be dressed. In *King Lear*, Edgar as Mad Tom, for instance, is dressed in nothing but rags, Lear enters at one point with a crown of flowers on his head and stage directions informs us that on her return to England Lear's exiled daughter is wearing armour. But about *Macbeth*? Other than carrying swords, there aren't any direct instructions about how the characters should be dressed. The lack of these instructions has allowed different directors to make radically different costume choices, from often rather unsubtly signalled feudal Scottishness – tartan, sporrans, kilts, or medieval equivalent, all round, as depicted in the image on the previous page from a nineteenth century production – to entirely modern dress, with Macbeth sometimes kitted out like a dapper Glaswegian crime lord. And you can spot a postmodernist version of *Macbeth* if the characters are dressed in different styles from different cultures and periods.

Research versions of the *Macbeth* witches and you'll find a vast range of interpretations. However, in contrast to the other characters, the text does provide specific embedded directions as to how the weird sisters should be portrayed. For example, Banquo describes them in some detail. The Witches are 'so withered and wild in their attire' that they 'look not like th' inhabitants o' the earth'. So, in other words, they are aged and physically shrunken, utterly uncivilized and also otherworldly, the latter characteristic further emphasized by Banquo wondering whether they are real of 'fantastical'. In addition, he notes that each one has a 'choppy finger', 'skinny lips' and that it is difficult to determine their sex: 'you should be women/ And yet your beards forbid me to interpret/ That you are so'.

For a Jacobean audience, such distinctive features would confirm that the weird sisters are indeed witches. Witches in this period were conceived to be women who had forsaken their essential female identities in order to do the devil's work. Witches blood and skin were thought to become hardened, their sexual organs shrivelled and infertile, their breasts to lose the capacity to produce milk. Loss of these outward female characteristics also, of  course, makes tangible the inner loss of archetypally feminine virtues, such as kindness, mercy, gentleness and submissiveness to male authority.

———

31

Clearly Shakespeare wishes the audience to make a link between the bearded witches and Lady Macbeth, who infamously unsexes herself, a connection that feeds into the play's interrogation of deviant females and of masculinity.

Lighting

Lighting can be used starkly and boldly, such as in picking out a main character in a bright spotlight, or it can be used more subtly to convey mood and generate atmosphere. Intense white light makes everything look stark. Blue lights help to create a sense of coolness, whereas yellows, oranges and reds generate a sense of warmth and even passion. Floor lights can light an actor from beneath, making them look powerful and threatening. Light coming down on them from above can cause an actor to look vulnerable and threatened, or even angelic. Changes of lighting between scenes are common ways of changing the pervasive atmosphere.

However, for most of his theatrical career, Shakespeare was writing for the Globe theatre where performances took place only during daylight hours. Only when his plays were performed at the indoor theatre at Blackfriars, from around 1608, could Shakespeare employ lighting effects. Yet *Macbeth* is a play with a very distinctively dark, gloomy, ominous atmosphere. Indeed, once the play's action moves to the Macbeth's castle the atmosphere grows increasingly sinister, almost palpably thickening into a claustrophobic darkness. For a modern theatre or film director creating this oppressive atmosphere using lighting would be simple enough. But what about on the Globe stage?

In an article on the excellent British Library website, *Discovering Shakespeare*[5] John Mullan comments that Macbeth is a 'play where darkness had to be theatrically conjured rather than literally provided'. Mullan notes that, though Shakespeare may have used fireworks to create the 'lightning' accompanying the Witches [and perhaps also smoke for the 'fog and filthy air'] the playwright had no theatrical means of generating darkness other than through the play's

---

[5] www.bl.uk/shakespeare/articles/conjuring-darkness-in-macbeth.

dialogue and imagery.

As we have already noted, torches are carried in several scenes to indicate the night time setting. In addition, the characters themselves frequently comment on the light or the absence of light. In the first scene, for example, the Witches say they will meet with Macbeth 'ere the set of sun' and refer to the air around them as foggy and 'filthy'. Of course, Macbeth and Lady Macbeth also evoke darkness in many of their speeches, from Macbeth's 'let not light see my black and deep desires' to his wife's 'come, thick night', which is later echoed by Macbeth's 'come, seeling Night'. Indeed, Lady Macbeth before her death tries desperately to erase and to escape the darkness she has called into being.

More subtly, as Mullan explains, darkness is implied by how characters address each other, particularly during the tensest scenes, i.e. those dealing with the darkest deeds. For example, in Act II Scene 1, when Macbeth enters he is greeted by Banquo with a terse and wary 'Who's there?'. Similarly, in the following scene, after Duncan's murder, before he re-enters their private chamber, Macbeth nervously calls out 'Who's there – what, ho!', even though it is likely that only his wife would be there. Mullan points out that the original Jacobean audience would be able to clearly see the actors even when the characters are supposedly not meant to. What, though, might have been the dramatic effect of this disjuncture between what the Globe audience saw and heard?

Could a more powerful dramatic effect be created by darkness in daylight than could be achieved by more literal modern atmospheric lighting? Possibly. The Globe audience seeing what the characters cannot see makes it seem as if the world of the play, and all the characters therein, is locked into some form of universal, essentially psychological, darkness, a blindness so intense that characters cannot even recognise what is palpably there before them. And if they cannot recognise concrete, physical objects, what chance have they of uncovering hidden desires, subtle plots and dark deceptions? And this unnatural, perceptual darkness aligns neatly with one of the play's major themes, the difficulty of distinguishing reality from illusion.

Music & sound effects

Music is a highly effective device for developing mood and atmosphere. In Arthur Miller's play, *A View from the Bridge*, for instance, a romantic popular song, 'Paper-Doll' is played while two young lovers dance together in front of a man who absolutely detests and opposes their relationship, and a charged, threatening atmosphere is immediately generated. In another of Miller's plays, *Death of a Salesman* a flute is used as a leitmotiv for the dreaminess of the central character Willy Loman. In *Hamlet*, Ophelia's madness is signalled by her singing of subversive and bawdy songs and Shakespeare weaves music into many of his comedies.

A modern film maker could, of course, provide a suitably atmospheric soundtrack for a film of *Macbeth*. In contrast, it is unlikely that Shakespeare would have employed many musicians for productions of this plays - by all accounts, the bard was a canny businessman and kept a keen eye on the finances of productions. Sound effects would also have been limited, though, as we've said, Shakespeare creates spectacular special effects through his language. There are, however, a few points in the play when specific stage directions indicate sound effects and/ musical accompaniment.

- Thunder

Each time the Witches appear there is a stage direction for thunder. Clearly, if loud enough, the sound of thunder can itself be frightening, particularly to audience members with a delicate constitution, and obviously, symbolically, thunder is always ominous. Storms and thunder in Shakespeare's plays also indicate disorder and disharmony, either presaging or echoing some sort of breach of the natural order. Probably the sound of thunder would have been created at the Globe through the use of fireworks.

Other sound effects used to ratchet up the tension include drums, a bell, an owl and insistent 'knocking'. Before Macbeth chances upon the Witches in Act I Scene 3, we hear a 'drum within' and the same militaristic association is employed near the end of the play when Mentieth and other Lords are shown rallying near Dunsinane. As with various other elements of plays, live, on stage, drumming can be very powerful and dramatic in a way that it's difficult to imagine when just reading the stage direction on the page. A 'bell rings' during the night as Macbeth is stealing towards Duncan's chamber to commit regicide. Macbeth himself explains the symbolism – 'it is a knell', suggesting a deep, sombre and atmospheric tolling. Soon after this, waiting alone for her husband to return from the murder scene, Lady Macbeth is startled by 'the owl that shrieked'. Once again, the significance is made explicit, connecting the ill omen of the owl's shriek to the 'fatal bellman', i.e. the man who rang the bell before an execution.

- Multiple flourishes of trumpets and hautboys

As we've mentioned, the celebratory golden-sound of trumpets is associated with Duncan and later with Malcolm, while the ominously gloomy hautboys are entirely connected with Macbeth. In the play's final scene the action is topped and tailed by a 'flourish' of trumpets that signals order has been restored. Or at least, it has from Malcolm's perspective.

- Alarms and alarums

Probably a brief blast of as many musical instruments as possible, it's hard to imagine precisely what these noises would be, but clearly they signify a call-to-arms and make the audience anticipate the onset of fighting. Macduff calls them 'clamorous harbingers of blood and death'.

- Various witches' chants and songs.

Shakespeare's instructions for the Witches' music and dance are rather sketchy. There's reference to a song, 'Come away, come away' and to another labelled 'Black Spirits', but no other details. The last time the Witches are on stage the direction merely says 'Music. The witches dance'. For the first two examples Shakespeare may have had particular songs in mind, but, clearly, there's plenty of scope for a director to decide how to present these musical interludes. Unsurprisingly, the dancing is often cut.

Dialogue & conversational analysis

Conversational analysis is a branch of discourse analysis used in linguistics to analyse patterns of meaning-making in human conversation. Although conversational analysis is conventionally applied to real conversations between real people in the real world, it can be easily and usefully applied to literary texts, especially to dialogue in novels and plays. Conversational analysis makes explicit the significance of underlying features of everyday conversational behaviour, such as variations in the length of contributions by speakers, modes of address and politeness terms, topic control and relevance, turn-taking, interruptions, asking and answering questions and truth telling. Often conversational analysis brings to our attention sub-textual issues of power and status between interlocutors.

Think, for example, of a situation where the power and status relationships are explicit and obvious, such as a classroom. If you were to read a transcript of a lesson, how would you know that the teacher was in control, presuming the teacher was in control? Firstly, of all the potential speakers in the class, probably the teacher will speak the most and with fewest interruptions from others. Secondly, the teacher will probably speak first and last, opening and closing the lesson/ discourse. We would also expect that the teacher to be in control of the topic, to set the agenda of any discussions and that she or he would ask questions which the pupils are expected to answer. In a situation where the teacher asks something like 'so how many people read Act III for homework as asked?' and a pupil answers with something like, 'I ate all the bananas, because I really like bananas' we can readily see this isn't the appropriate response and the teacher's authority may be being challenged.

We'll apply aspects of conversational analysis when we examine key scenes from each Act later in this book. For now, we'll sketch-out how the method can reveal underlying patterns by taking a quick look at Macbeth's first conversation with his wife in Act I Scene 5.

Lady Macbeth has just finished her 'unsex me here' soliloquy when Macbeth enters the room. Notice how she immediately takes the lead, speaking first. She has five lines before Macbeth is allowed, or able, to respond, by which time she has already firmly established the topic of the ensuing conversation. Moreover, she addresses her husband in terms of both his old and new status: 'Great Glamis! Worthy Cawdor!'. And yet, she also addresses him as an equal, using the familiar [rather than the respectful] second person pronoun 'thy'. In contrast, Macbeth addresses his wife in tender, loving terms, 'my dearest love'. His turn is just seven words before his wife asks him a question: 'And when goes hence?' Significantly, Lady Macbeth doesn't return the affectionate address. Macbeth obediently answers her question. The arrangement of the lines on the page also suggests that either Lady Macbeth twice interrupts her husband, completing his line, or that, at least, her words come hard-on-the-heels of his. Only another four words from him and then Lady Macbeth's dominance of this short interaction is underlined by the longest speech in extract, lasting ten lines.

In her speech beginning 'O! never shall sun that morrow see!' Lady Macbeth characteristically uses declaratives, such as the sentence above, as well as imperatives 'To beguile the time...' Clearly, she is the one in command. Even her declarative sentences function as imperatives: 'you shall put / This night's great business into my despatch'. She uses the second-person pronoun to address her husband and a powerful modal verb 'shall'. In contrast, Macbeth responds with the third person plural, 'we' and the less powerful modal 'will'. Again, his final response is short and his line is completed as if eagerly by his wife. And again she is in imperiously imperative mode 'look up'; 'leave all'. Lady Macbeth finishes her speech and simultaneously closes the scene, with an incomplete line that lands tellingly on its final first-person pronoun 'me'.

The nature of the play

What is a tragedy?

According to *The Complete A-Z English Literature Handbook* a tragedy is a 'drama which ends disastrously' and falls into two broad types:

- Greek tragedy, where fate brings about the downfall of the character(s).
- Shakespearean tragedy, where a character has free will and their fatal flaw causes the downfall.

As you shall discover when you read our essay on the tragic protagonist of *Macbeth* the second half of that second point is much disputed by literary academics and Shakespeare scholars. And, in fact, it seems that the description above of a Greek tragedy fits *Macbeth* quite snugly.

According to Jennifer Wallace in *The Cambridge Introduction to Tragedy*, 'Tragedy is an art form created to confront the most difficult experiences we face; death, loss, injustice, thwarted passion, despair.' Wallace goes on to explain that 'questions about the causes of suffering, which are raised in each culture, are posed powerfully in tragedy.'[6] That's helpful, but couldn't we say the same sorts of things about the academic subject of philosophy?

---

[6] Wallace, *The Cambridge Introduction to Tragedy*.

While, on the one hand, there are critics, such as Terry Eagleton, who argue the only thing that the plays we call tragedies have in common is that they are 'very, very sad', on the other hand, many other critics argue that all literary tragedies share distinctive common formal features which separate them from real-life stories of unhappiness. And, if we shrink our perspective down from tragedies as a whole art form to Shakespeare's versions, we'll discover there's not much academic agreement either about what attributes these plays share:

'An eminent Shakespearian scholar famously remarked that there is no such thing as Shakespearian Tragedy; there are only Shakespearian tragedies'.

So begins Tom McAlindon's essay *What is a Shakespearian Tragedy?*[7] The author goes on to point out how attempts to define tragedy, such as those we've quoted above, tend to 'give a static impression of the genre and incline towards prescriptivism', ignoring the fact that genres are constantly changing and developing over time.

So, to sum up: The definition of 'tragedy' is hotly contested. So too is the definition of Shakespearian Tragedy. Indeed, more fundamentally the idea of defining both these terms is itself contested within literary criticism. So where does that leave us with *Macbeth*? Lost somewhere within the fog and filthy air it seems. Perhaps a sensible way to try to find a route out of the academic fogginess is to start at the beginning and then navigate our way from that fixed point. In terms of defining tragedy as an art form, Aristotle's theories of tragedy serve well as a starting point.

Aristotle

Often it is assumed that Aristotle was setting down a prescriptivist rule book for writing tragedies, a kind of classical instruction manual for aspiring playwrights to slavishly follow. This assumption is mistaken. In fact, Aristotle, in his *Poetics*, was describing the features of classical tragedies as he saw them. Taken as prescriptivist or descriptivist, what is certain is that Aristotle's

---

[7] McAllindon, *The Cambridge Companion to Tragedy*, p.1.

ideas about tragedies have been hugely influential. In particular, four key ideas have helped shape the ways tragedies have been written and read for hundreds of years. These ideas concern:

i.   the nature of the protagonist
ii.   the cause of tragic action
iii. the significance of plot
iv.   the emotional effect of tragedy on an audience.

For our purposes, the first two of these concepts are particularly interesting.

The protagonist in classical tragedy is always high-born, a prince or king or someone of equivalent status. This means their fall is as precipitous and dramatic as possible - right from the top to the very bottom of society - in a way that the fall of someone from the bottom to the bottom of society would not be. As the tragic hero or heroine is high-born and they fall a long way, the impact is immense, sending shockwaves out across the whole world of the play, creating cracks and fissures in the social fabric. Think of an elephant falling from the top of the Empire State Building, perhaps. Crucially, the primary cause of the fall is a fault in the tragic protagonist. Historically Shakespearian critics often conceived of the tragic flaw, or hamartia, in psychological terms, but according to Aristotle it could equally be a terrible decision made by the tragic hero.

Read through an Aristolean critical perspective, *Macbeth* is a play fundamentally about its titular hero, whose tragic fall is precipitated by his hamartia. Different critics argue about what this hamartia might be – trusting the Witches, being persuaded by his wife, committing regicide – but many have plumped for his 'vaulting ambition'. In this sense, character becomes fate, and this collapses the distinction between Greek and Shakespearian tragedy with which we started. Wrapped within the overall tragedy is another sub-genre: though the main plot of *Macbeth* doesn't feature revenge, the Malcolm and Macduff sub-plots do, so, to this extent the play also has features in common with revenge tragedies.

Modern criticism

However, most modern Shakespearian critics argue that an Aristolean approach to tragedy over-emphasises the importance of the tragic hero and of characters in general. These critics are more interested in the role of society and of history in shaping the experience of characters. Read through this kind of framework, the tragedy stems from irresolvable, conflicting forces within the period in which Shakespeare was writing, a period that historians call the early modern. So, for instance, a modern critic might argue that *Macbeth* stages a conflict between traditional, essential feudal values – of loyalty, duty, honour and so forth – and a new Renaissance spirit of individualism and self-determination that inspires characters to take decisive action and shape their own destinies. And this critical insight helps us to see how *Macbeth* links to other plays from the period, especially Christopher Marlowe's *Doctor Faustus*.

Doctor Faustus

Throughout the early part of his career Shakespeare seems to have been in keen competition with Marlowe and there are many parallels between their

plays. In *Doctor Faustus* [1592] Marlowe dramatized the story of an Elizabethan intellectual, a proto-scientist, driven by the dynamic new spirit of adventure and ambition to uncover all the secrets of the world. A laudable ambition we might agree, and one that still drives scientific discoveries to this day. However, Faustus'

ambition is so all-consuming that he is prepared to give everything he has to know everything, even his immortal soul. Tempted by the demon Mephistopheles, Faustus makes a pact to exchange his soul for limitless knowledge. The consequences for Faustus are, naturally, not pleasant.

Macbeth shares with Marlowe's play the demonic element. However, in Shakespeare's play the Witches replace Mephistopheles. Shakespeare's protagonist may be a man-of-action, rather than a thinker, but, like Faustus, he is also tempted into transgression by mysterious and supernatural forces, and also suffers the horrible consequences. There's also the framework of the medieval morality plays underpinning both more modern dramas. Of Shakespeare's tragedies, *Macbeth* has a peculiarly dark, oppressive, almost nightmarish atmosphere. And this is another feature it also has in common with Marlowe's play.

Several critics have also noted how the action of *Macbeth* seems simultaneously to move forward at a fair lick, with lots of relatively short, quick scenes, especially in comparison to the other tragedies, and yet it is a play also characterised by a pervading sense of stasis. It is almost as if a spell has fallen over the central characters, the Macbeths, who are 'locked in an interim', 'a perpetual nightmarish present' out of which they cannot seem to escape. Here, for example, is Laurie E. Maguire on the subject:

'The play is characterised by frantic speed… Once launched on a life of crime, Macbeth acts speedily and decisively to eliminate Banquo, kill Fleance, visit the Witches. However, these kinetic images and hasty actions are countered by an emotional freeze-frame as the Macbeths become imprisoned in affective stasis… With Macbeth's bloody images and his wife's flashbacks, the couple remain on a temporal treadmill.'[8]

As you will discover as you read through this guide, modern critics have also been very interested in how masculinity and power are presented in *Macbeth* and often critics see these themes as the play's central concerns. Other critics, such as Emma Smith[9], are interested in moral culpability and questions of agency in the play, concerns which takes us neatly back to Wallace's attempts to define the nature of tragedy.

---

[8] Maguire, *Studying Shakespeare*, p.133.

[9] Smith, *This is Shakespeare*.

The big themes

Appearance and reality

The theme of appearance versus reality - the awareness that things are not really what they seem to be and what we perceive to be reality frequently fails to correspond with the truth - preoccupied Shakespeare throughout his entire writing career. It was as central to his early comedies such as *The Comedy of Errors* and *A Midsummer Night's Dream* as it was to the late romances, such as *The Winter's Tale* and *The Tempest*. In *Macbeth*, the theme of appearance versus reality is introduced by the Witches in Scene I through the paradoxical 'fair is foul and foul is fair'. Not only do their enigmatic words suggest the moral uncertainty and confusion that runs throughout the play and hint at how what appears to be one thing on the surface might actually hide its opposite quality beneath, they also imply a fundamental instability and duplicity within language itself. The ways in which we can be deceived by appearances is further developed in Scene II with the revelation concerning the Thane of Cawdor's deceptive treachery, a man on whom Duncan had 'built an absolute trust'. Duncan admits, in Scene IV, 'There's no art / To find the mind's construction in the face', acknowledging the impossibility of ever really being able to discern someone's true inner nature from the outward persona they present to the world. Having learnt this lesson from the first Thane of Cawdor's betrayal, it is ironic and arguably foolish that Duncan then goes on to make the same mistake of putting his trust in Macbeth by making him the next Thane of Cawdor, only to be betrayed and murdered by him.

Our human susceptibility to being deceived by outward appearances is

something Lady Macbeth seeks to exploit in her advice to Macbeth to 'look like th'innocent flower / But be the serpent under't'. She urges Macbeth to act the part of a welcoming and dutiful host towards Duncan, while at the same time plotting to kill the king. The deception is intended to lure Duncan into a false sense of security and make him more vulnerable, while also diverting suspicion away from the Macbeths.

Artfully Shakespeare captures the incongruity between appearance and reality in Lady Macbeth's use of figurative language and the subtle shift between simile and metaphor. While Macbeth is only *like* a flower, he *is* to be a serpent. Shakespeare's audience would also have recognised in Lady Macbeth's words  an allusion to a medal that had been made to celebrate the discovery of the Gunpowder Plot and the attempt to assassinate James I by blowing up the Houses of Parliament. The medal depicted a serpent hiding among flowers. By alluding to it here, Shakespeare draws a deliberate parallel between the Macbeths and the gunpowder plotters; both behind a veneer of loyalty and respectability both were plotting regicide. Lady Macbeth's use of double meanings in the next few lines further emphasises the gap between appearances and reality. When she tells Macbeth 'He's that coming / Must be provided for, and you shall put / This night's great business into my dispatch', she demonstrates the duplicitous potential within language and the potential for ambiguity of meaning to be exploited for contrary purposes: 'Provided for' could mean feeding or killing Duncan, while 'business' could mean the act of feasting or murder and 'dispatch' could mean welcoming Duncan or killing him. While a servant who overhears her words would therefore interpret one level of meaning, Macbeth would decipher the deeper and darker implications to her words.

Shakespeare also uses plot structure to emphasise the dangers of trusting appearances. Duncan arrives at Macbeth's castle in scene VI straight after Lady Macbeth's speech to her husband encouraging duplicity. Duncan's praise of the castle for its 'pleasant seat' and air that 'nimbly and sweetly recommends itself' increases the sense of dramatic irony, as we know this is the place where the Macbeths are plotting to murder him. Banquo's awkward praise for the castle as a place where the martlet makes it home sounds like he is trying to convince himself against his better judgement of Duncan's safety. Again the double meaning of language, in words such as 'haunting', 'heaven's breath', 'haunt' and 'delicate', could imply a deathly reality beneath the castle's pleasant façade. Moreover, the word 'martlet', while signifying a housemartin, in Shakespeare's time also meant someone who was easily duped and deceived.

Macbeth is another character fully aware of the potential distance between appearances and reality, though he is not as accomplished as his wife at disguising his intentions. In Act I Scene 4, after hearing Duncan pronounce Malcolm the Prince of Cumberland and heir to the throne - therefore blocking Macbeth's passage to the kingship he has been promised by the Witches - Macbeth is desperate to conceal his murderous thoughts from his fellow nobles, imploring the stars to 'hide your fires, / Let not light see my black and deep desires'. Equally concerned about Macbeth's difficulty in hiding his true feelings from others, Lady Macbeth tells him 'Your face, my thane, is as a book where men / May read strange matters'. Immediately following the discovery of Duncan's murdered body, Macbeth struggles to maintain the pretence of a shocked and innocent subject. Fearing the truth will be discovered, he kills the guards who were to be blamed for the murder. His justification to the others for his actions is so artificial and unconvincing that Lady Macbeth is forced to take action and feign fainting to distract everyone's attention before suspicion falls on her husband.

As the play develops, Macbeth learns from his wife the art of hiding the truth through surface appearances. He successfully questions Banquo about his whereabouts in order to plan his murder without either Banquo or even Lady Macbeth suspecting Macbeth's true motives. In Act III Scene Two, in response to his wife's anxiety about his dark mood and how it might be interpreted by his guests at the coronation banquet, Macbeth reassures her how they must 'make our faces vizards [masks] to our hearts, / Disguising what they are', which parallels her earlier advice to him to 'look like the innocent flower'. Even at the banquet, before the unsettling news that Fleance has escaped, Macbeth boasts how 'Our self will mingle with society, / and play the humble host'. In this line Shakespeare uses one of his favourite metaphors - that life itself is like a play in which we are actors who have to perform our parts, some more successfully than others. Macbeth will play the role of generous and care-free host, disguising the underlying reality that he is a tyrant waiting for news of Banquo and Fleance's murder. However, the façade is soon broken with news of Fleance's escape, leading later in the play to Macbeth's guilty conscience manifesting itself in the form of Banquo's ghost.

As Lady Macbeth also learns by the end of the play, however strong the will, a guilty conscience cannot be suppressed indefinitely beneath the appearance of innocence. Not at least without serious damage to the psyche, as evinced through Macbeth's ghostly visions and Lady Macbeth's sleepwalking and eventual suicide. For Macbeth, after the banquet, the appearance of innocence and normality is forever shattered, with knowledge of his involvement in Duncan and Banquo's murder now widespread among his subjects, as alluded to by Lennox's sarcastic words at the end of Act III that 'The gracious Duncan / Was pitied of Macbeth - marry, he was dead. / And the right-valiant Banquo walked too late'.

Macbeth's failure to disguise the true self that lies beneath his public persona is also evident in the clothing imagery used by Angus in Act V Scene 2. Angus describes how Macbeth must now 'feel his title / Hang loose around him, like a giant's robe / Upon a dwarfish thief'. Likening Macbeth to a 'dwarfish thief' that has stolen his clothes from a 'giant', the simile emphasises how Macbeth is an illegitimate ruler who has usurped the role from the rightful king, Duncan, and now lacks the moral stature to perform his duties. Macbeth is no longer able to use the appearance of kingship to disguise the reality of his inner nature from his subjects and, consequently, his authority and control over them rapidly evaporates.

While Macbeth is ultimately unable to convince his subjects that the appearance he conveys is the truth, ironically, he is himself brought down by his inability to distinguish between truth and appearance, as evidenced by his interaction with the Witches. When he returns to visit them in Act IV Scene 1, the apparitions' prophecies to Macbeth that 'none of woman born shall harm Macbeth' and 'Macbeth shall never vanquished be until / Great Birnam Wood to high Dunsinane hill shall come' lures him into a false sense of security. Not until Act V, when he sees the branches carried by the soldiers advancing towards his castle and, facing Macduff, discovers that his opponent was born from a caesarean section, does Macbeth realise the duplicitous ambiguity of the apparitions' words that hide truth behind appearance. As he tells the messenger who informs him the woods are beginning to move in Act V Scene 5, 'I pull in resolution and begin / To doubt the equivocation of the fiend /

That lies like truth.' Only now is he able to distinguish between appearance and reality and see the wood from the trees, so to speak. The reference to equivocation - the practice of exploiting the ambiguity of meaning within words in order to disguise the truth without technically lying - would also have reminded Shakespeare's audience of the Gunpowder Plot and, in particular, the Jesuit priest Father Garnet who used equivocation to conceal his knowledge of the conspiracy and became known as 'the great equivocator'.

The theme of appearance versus reality within the play therefore becomes framed within the wider historical context of the attempted assassination of the new king, James I. In *Macbeth* Shakespeare seems to imply that the destruction and damnation of equivocators who hid the truth behind appearances in order to take the king's life. As the porter, who symbolically imagines himself as 'porter of hell-gate', declares, 'here's an equivocator...who committed treason enough for God's sake, yet could not equivocate to heaven. O, come in, equivocator'.

If there is a moment of anagnorisis in *Macbeth* - the moment in all tragedies where the hero realises the truth of their inner nature – arguably it occurs for Macbeth straight after the suicide of his wife. His realisation that life is 'a poor player / That struts and frets his hour upon the stage / And then is heard no more' or the realisation that life is 'a tale / told by an idiot, full of sound and fury, / Signifying nothing' seems to peer behind the appearance of all things to arrive at the fundamental reality that there is no meaning to life. Here, Shakespeare again deploys one of his most common metaphors of life as play, where we are all just bad actors who have not learnt our lines. Fumbling around on stage, waiting for the final curtain to bring it all to an end, we don't even know our parts. While it is tempting to take Macbeth's view of life as meaningless and pointless as the play's final comment on appearance versus reality, it is important to note that the play does not stop there. And neither does Macbeth. Although Macbeth does not live to see it, meaning and order are restored at the end of the play and life goes on. Perhaps we should see Macbeth's nihilistic view of reality as expressed here not as the final judgement on life, but yet another example of one of its many deceitful appearances. To say that life has no meaning is, paradoxically, to give life meaning, even if that meaning is a negative one. Instead, perhaps Shakespeare is suggesting that there is no absolute reality behind appearances, but, rather, just an infinite number of parts to play. Macbeth, after all, plays a variety of roles throughout the play, even if some of these were unwisely chosen. This fluidity of meaning is in itself ultimately liberating. It means we are also free to choose the role we wish to play and to create our own meanings. Or, as Macduff puts it in the closing scene, 'the time is free'.

Kingship

What makes a good king? How should kings be chosen? Is it ever justifiable to remove a king from power? These are all important questions taken up and explored by Shakespeare in *Macbeth*. In doing so, Shakespeare engages in contemporary debates around kingship that were particularly relevant at the time of writing the play, given a new king, James I, had recently been crowned in England and had himself written two books on the theme of kingship, *The True Law of Free Monarchies* and *Basilikon Doron*. In these works, James set forward his belief in the Divine Right of Kings, the theory that God choses a nation's king to rule over the kingdom as his representative, or as James writes, kings 'sit upon God his throne in the earth and have the count of their administration unto him'. An attack against the king is therefore an attack against God. James also outlined the characteristics of a good king which included being rational and calm rather than overly emotional, caring about his people, respecting and following church law and not being selfish or motivated by personal ambition. In contrast, according to James, a bad king or tyrant acted out of emotion rather than reason, was only interested in themselves and personal ambition, showed no loyalty to others, was manipulative and villainous, used violence to gain power and fear to control their subjects. Throughout *Macbeth*, Shakespeare generally upholds James' ideas about kingship with one important exception: while James argues that no king, even a tyrant, should ever be removed by the people, as even a bad king was chosen by God to test and refine his people, Shakespeare seems to suggest that under certain circumstances, the removal of a tyrant is sometimes necessary for the good of a nation.

Duncan is the first king to appear in the play and possesses many positive personal attributes. He commands the respect and loyalty of most of his subjects; warriors like Macbeth and Banquo are willing to risk their lives protecting him. He is magnanimous, rewarding Macbeth for his bravery in the battle and bestowing him with the title Thane of Cawdor. Macbeth himself acknowledges how Duncan is humble and has performed his offices as king well, musing in his soliloquy at the start of Act I Scene 7 where he decides against killing Duncan how 'this Duncan / Hath borne his faculties so meek, hath been / So clear in his great office'. Most importantly, as Macbeth implies when he considers how Duncan's 'virtues / Will plead like angels,' Duncan is God's divinely appointed king, chosen by God to rule Scotland. Deposing Duncan is therefore an act of defiance and open rebellion against God's will and purposes. This is why, when Duncan is murdered, the whole of natural order is affected due to the disruption caused to God's Great Chain of Being. James described how a rebellion against God's king was 'monstrous and unnatural' and as a result of Duncan's murder, unnatural events start to occur such as a mousing owl killing a falcon or Duncan's horses eating each other as reported by Ross and the old man in Act II Scene 4, immediately following Duncan's murder.

Despite Duncan's many admirable qualities and being God's divinely appointed king, he is, from a Jacobean perspective, a weak king. At the start of the play his kingdom is destabilised by invaders from the outside and traitors from within. He is a poor judge of character and too trusting, building 'an absolute trust' on the first Thane of Cawdor who turns out to be a traitor who plots against him, only to then place his trust in the next Thane of Cawdor, Macbeth, who brutally murders him at the first opportunity. He is also overly reliant on warriors like Macbeth and Banquo to fight his battles; along with Henry VI, Duncan is the only king in all of Shakespeare's plays who does not lead his own men into battle. His position is further weakened and destabilized by the system of royal succession in feudal Scotland, where kingship was not decided by primogeniture but by tanistry – a system in which a new king is appointed by nomination. By being forced to promote men like Macbeth to higher noble positions for the violence they wield on behalf of the crown, Duncan unwittingly stokes the ambition that leads to Macbeth coveting the throne, a position that would be unattainable for him if succession was a matter of biological lineage exclusively. And within this context, Duncan's decision to nominate his son as the Prince of Northumberland and future heir to the throne so soon after the battle to save his kingship was won by Macbeth, seems like an unwise and provocative snub to the hero of the hour.

Duncan is also portrayed as an effeminate king, too gentle and womanly according to the stereotypical conventions of Shakespeare's day. In Macbeth's dagger soliloquy, the murder is represented as a rape, with Macbeth as Tarquin and Duncan feminised as Lucretia, while after death Duncan's corpse is described as 'a new gorgon', a woman from Greek mythology with snakes for hair and the power to turn anyone who looked at her into stone, implying that Duncan was a failed patriarchal and fatherly ruler, falling short of James' ideal that the king 'is truly the politic father of his people.'

While Duncan is an example of a morally good but politically weak king, Macbeth, in contrast, is a clear example of a tyrant. He uses violence and deceit to cruelly murder the innocent and defenceless Duncan in his bed, motivated by base ambition and lust for power; he is also acting in direct defiance of divine will having forcibly removed God's chosen king. In the light of the recent Gunpowder plot against James I, it was necessary for Shakespeare to condemn the evils of regicide and demonstrate the dire consequences that would follow such an evil act. Having seized power through illegitimate means, Macbeth is forced to maintain his power through ever increasing violence and fear, first through the cowardly assassination of his best friend and then, even more shockingly, through the murder of Macduff's innocent wife and children. The evil of Macbeth's rule is accentuated by Shakespeare in the unnatural events that occur in the natural world after the death of Duncan, and in the imagery of darkness, sickness and blood that pervades the play. This is evident in Macbeth's invocation to 'Come, seeling night, Scarf up the tender eye of pitiful day' after he orders Banquo's death, or in his later realisation after the appearance of Banquo's ghost that 'blood will have blood' and 'I am in blood / stepped in so far that should I wade no more, / Returning were as tedious as go o'er'.

The language of Hell and damnation permeates the whole play, suggesting God's retribution against Macbeth's subversion of the Divine Right of Kings, such as in the Porter's reference to himself as 'porter of hell-gate' after the murder of Duncan, or Macduff's reference to Macbeth as a 'hell-kite' after he learns of his family's murder. The imagery of damnation also links to the motif of sleeplessness that also recurs throughout the play, such as in the almost schizophrenic, auditory hallucination that Macbeth hears before the murder of Duncan, telling him 'Sleep no more, / Macbeth does murder sleep', which suggests the fracturing of Macbeth's psyche under the weight of his guilty conscience, loss of inner peace and forfeiture of eternal salvation. Shakespeare uses another motif to comment on Macbeth's despotic reign, that of clothing, such as in Angus' mocking of Macbeth that 'Now does he feel his title / hang loose about  him, like a giant's robe / upon a dwarfish thief', which reinforces the illegitimacy of Macbeth's Kingship and his unsuitability to fulfil the role of God's king.

The consequences of Macbeth's usurpation are also keenly felt in the land itself. James in his *The True Law of Free Monarchies* adopted the classical analogy of the body politic that compared society with a human body, arguing that the king was 'the head of this microcosm of the body of man…preventing all evil that may come to the body or any part thereof'. It therefore follows that any sickness in the head will be felt throughout the whole body. We see this in *Macbeth* in the many images of sickness and disease that Shakespeare uses to describe Scotland, infected as it is by the tyranny of Macbeth's ungodly rule. Just as Macbeth is afflicted by his 'heat-oppressed brain' and experiences fevered hallucinations that 'might appal the devil', Scotland itself is described by Ross as a 'grave' filled with 'sighs and groans and shrieks', while Macbeth pleads with the doctor in Act V to 'cast / The water of my land, find her disease, / And purge it to a sound and pristine health'. Macbeth does not realise that it is his own bloody, tyrannical and illegitimate reign that is the cause of Scotland's sickness, and only the restoration of a legitimate and divinely appointed king can restore her to health.

The fulfilment of the Witches' prophecy of Birnam Wood moving to Dunsinane when the soldiers use the branches as camouflage in Act V can be seen as a symbolic act of the land and nature itself rising up against the unnatural tyranny of Macbeth's illegitimate reign. Only when Macbeth is defeated and his tyrannical reign ended can health and well-being be restored to Scotland.

The third and final Scottish king we see in *Macbeth* is Malcolm, who, as Duncan's son, represents the legitimate and divinely approved heir to the throne according to the system of primogeniture favoured in England. Malcolm plays a small part earlier in the play: He is nominated 'Prince of Cumberland' and heir to the throne by Duncan in Act I; then, in Act II, he flees to England after Duncan's murder. He reappears in Act IV Scene 3, a quite long-winded scene that considerably slows down the action of the play, but which performs an important function in presenting Malcolm as a model of the ideal Jacobean king, although it is not until the end of the play that he actually receives the crown. Malcolm's testing of Macduff's loyalty to Scotland in the scene by pretending to be even more selfish, immoral and tyrannical then Macbeth, shows how he possesses the Machiavellian qualities of kingship admired by Jacobeans and does not share the naïve, overly trusting nature of his father. Only when the disgusted Macduff withdraws his support from Duncan - therefore convincing Malcolm of Macduff's true loyalty to Scotland - does Malcolm reveal the truth of his noble character, as someone who has sacrificed all of his personal desires to the service of his people. Malcolm assures Macduff that 'What I am truly, / Is thine and my poor country's to command'. Malcolm's moral perfection is established though his revelation that he has never before lied, been envious of others or betrayed anyone, telling Macduff he 'never was forsworn' and 'would not betray / The devil to his fellow, and delight / No less in truth than life'. This is in sharp contrast to Macbeth's immoral lies, betrayals and covetousness. Furthermore, the admission that 'I am yet / Unknown to woman' symbolically demonstrates how Duncan is free from the unnatural and corrupting maternal forces of the

Witches and Lady Macbeth that have undermined and emasculated Macbeth.

Alongside Macduff, who equally is free of feminine influence, being not 'one of woman born', Malcolm is presented to the audience as one able to re-establish the masculine, paternal authority of the king who, as James argued, served as his subjects' 'natural father and kindly master'. Though he appears not to actually fight, Malcolm also leads his army into battle in Act V, unlike his father who, in Act I was reliant on his nobles to defend Scotland. However, it is Macduff rather than Malcolm who must eventually kill Macbeth and end his 'watchful tryanny', which insulates Malcolm from the physical act of regicide. And it is on this final act of usurping a tyrant that Shakespeare's play appears to diverge from James' view of kingship. While James argued that a king, however oppressive and despotic they became, should never be deposed, as they were still chosen by God and could be used by God to test his people and strengthen their humility - it is the case that Macbeth was chosen and crowned king by the other Lords of Scotland in a lawfully binding ceremony - the ending of *Macbeth* suggests that the forcible removal of a tyrant is sometimes justified in order to restore a nation to peace and health. Shakespeare therefore subtly shifts the ground James' arguments about kingship by suggesting it is not just a matter of how a king comes to power that is important, but the means in which they choose to exercise that power, therefore challenging James' belief in absolute monarchy.

Manliness

One of the major questions Shakespeare explores in *Macbeth* is what does it mean to be a man? Within the violent, feudal society of medieval Scotland, masculinity is primarily defined through acts of strength and courage. Shakespeare establishes Macbeth's manly heroism though the captain's account of the battle in Act I Scene 2, where Macbeth is described as both 'brave' and 'valiant' for the way he single-handedly dispatches 'the merciless Macdonald'. However, the exaggeratedly macho description of Macbeth 'with his brandished steel, / which smoked with bloody execution' equates masculinity and heroism with an idealised and glamorised violence in a similar fashion to the way 1980s action films presented actors such as Sylvester Stallone and Arnold Schwarzenegger as muscle-clad warriors wielding oversized weapons and guns - phallic symbols of male power. Furthermore, the brutality of Macbeth's violence, where he 'unseamed [Macdonald] from the nave to th'chaps', while serving well in wartime, proves to be a problematic in peacetime; Duncan discovers that the violent forces released during the battle are beyond his control and are soon directed back against him when Macbeth murders him to seize the crown for himself.

Conversely, Lady Macbeth's anxiety over her husband is not how he will give expression to his violent masculinity in peacetime, but rather how the absence of war will expose his gentle and effeminate private self that lies beneath his public persona of a man of action. After reading his letter detailing the Witches' prophecies about becoming king, she immediately worries how 'I fear thy nature, / is too full o'th'milk of human kindness', comparing her husband to a nursing mother and fearing he possesses too much feminine compassion to murder the king. For Lady Macbeth, and the warrior culture of Scotland she is subjected to, true masculinity should be brutal and merciless. This is why she prays to evil spirits to 'unsex me here / And fill me from the crown to the toe topfull / Of direst cruelty'; she must somehow rid herself of the gentle feminine qualities idealised in women in Shakespeare's day and instead become like a man. Or at least, if she is to enable the savage and callous act of regicide, to become what society tells her are the essential qualities of manliness.

When Macbeth initially refuses to go through with the murder in Act I Scene 7, it is his perceived lack of stereotypical masculine qualities that she attacks. Accusingly, she tells him 'when you durst do it, then you were a man'. Lady Macbeth successfully manipulates her husband into murder, despite his plea that 'I dare do all that may become a man', by convincing him that the only way to prove his manliness and love for her is through killing Duncan. Moreover, it is her own renunciation of feminine, maternal qualities, signified through her shocking willingness to have 'dash'd the brains out' of her own baby that has presumably died in infancy, which finally wins Macbeth round to agreeing to kill the king and demonstrate his own masculine power to his wife. Arguably the phallic image of the dagger that Macbeth hallucinates in Act II Scene 1 that leads him towards Duncan's murder symbolises the masculine ideal of patriarchal power that Macbeth aspires to represent. Yet the unsubstantial and ephemeral nature of the hallucination also suggests its illusory nature. And when Macbeth loses control of his senses in the banquet scene as he hallucinates Banquo's ghost, it is his lack of manliness at which Lady Macbeth once again strikes, accusing him 'Are you a man?' and 'What, quite unmanned in folly?' His public expression of terror in this scene is at odds with the male ideal of courage and fearlessness that defines manliness within his society and therefore also undermines his power and authority as king.

It is perhaps surprising that Lady Macbeth so successfully exploits Macbeth's inadequate sense of masculinity, given his exploits as a soldier and reputation among his fellow men as a courageous hero, as evidenced at the start of the play. But we need to remember that in the culture of medieval, feudal Scotland, as well as in Shakespeare's England, male power and authority was demonstrated and confirmed through the ability to produce children - particularly sons. As the critic Coppelia Kahn suggests, 'sexually and socially, in Shakespeare's world, fatherhood validates a man's identity'[10]. Macbeth's childless state and failure to produce a male heir diminishes his status as a 'real man' in the eyes of his contemporaries and, specifically, in the eyes of his

_____

[10] Kahn, *Man's Estate: Masculine Identity in Shakespeare* p.183.

of his wife. His rivalry with his best friend, Banquo, caused by the Witches' prophecy that, while Macbeth will become king, Banquo's descendants will establish a line of kings, is exacerbated by Macbeth's childless state that contrasts with Banquo's paternal status. After his coronation as king, Macbeth determines to kill Banquo because he realises 'for Banquo's issue have I filed my mind'. He has murdered Duncan to make 'the seed of Banquo kings!'. His own enfeebled and emasculated state as a childless king is symbolised by his 'fruitless crown' and 'barren sceptre'. The inability to produce a male heir would have been seen as a weakness of kingship by Shakespeare's audience who were well aware of the uncertainties and instability experienced in England due to Queen Elizabeth I's lack of heir and natural successor. Arguably, Macbeth desires to kill Banquo and Fleance not only to prevent the Witches' prophecy from being fulfilled but also, subconsciously, to take revenge for his own childless state. His envy of Banquo's fatherhood is evident in his arguments used to stir up hatred for Banquo in the murderers he engages to kill him, where his description of Banquo as one whose 'issue' has 'beggared yours for ever' projects his own anxiety and jealousy concerning Banquo's children onto the murderers. Macbeth's repugnant and cowardly murder of Macduff's wife and children later on in the play can also be understood as a reaction to the apparition of Banquo's kingly line of descendants that the Witches show his in Act IV Scene 1, with the desire to eradicate Banquo's paternal status - which Macbeth realises is now impossible - is displaced onto Macduff.

As well as his failure to produce an heir - and therefore establish a patrilineal line of inheritance that patriarchal Jacobean society depended on for the maintenance of male rule and power through the inheritance of wealth, land, possessions and titles - Macbeth's masculinity is also called into question within the play by his unhealthy reliance upon women and consequent abdication of male authority. This is evident in his reaction to the Witches in Act I Scene 3. The Witches' unnatural and subversive femininity is manifested in the way their manly appearance challenges the clear gender divisions of Jacobean society. Banquo refuses to show any deference to them, despite his interest in their words, and asserts his independence and refusal to 'neither beg nor fear / You favours.' On the other hand, Macbeth becomes submissive in their presence, begging them to 'stay' and 'tell me more'. His male authority is completely undermined when he orders them to 'Speak, I charge you' to which they defiantly disappear. Their insidious influence over Macbeth is immediately detected by Banquo. Twice he comments how his 'partner's rapt', suggesting how Macbeth is now held captivated and entranced under the spell of the Witches' words. Even more destructive is the influence Macbeth allows his wife to exert over him, which, as we have already seen, convinces him to commit the grievous sin of regicide against his better judgement and despite his avowal that 'we will proceed no further in this business'. Lady Macbeth's own allusion to the biblical story of Adam and Eve in the advice to her husband to 'look like the innocent flower, / But be the serpent under't' also seems to hint at the catastrophic consequences that occur when a husband allows himself to be led astray by his wife.

Despite the many apparently misogynistic references to the dangers of female power in the play, it is possible to read the play as a critique of narrow interpretations of masculinity that lead to the oppression of women. The violence of Lady Macbeth's denial of femininity, where she is forced to pray to evil spirits to inhabit her and 'unsex' her, serves as an indictment of restrictive stereotypical views of gender that exclude women from power and autonomy and prove to be equally destructive for both sexes. Macduff's reaction to the murder of his family, where he responds to Malcolm's insensitive counsel to 'man-up' and 'dispute it like a man' with the impassioned admonition that 'I shall do so, / But I must also feel it like a man', further challenges the stereotypical view of men as being hard and unemotional that Lady Macbeth seems to have absorbed from her culture. By making such a move, the play momentarily starts to challenge and break down some of the binary oppositions that construct a rigid definition of gender within Shakespeare's society. However, the ending of the play seems to uphold a traditional, patriarchal view of power. Male order and authority as represented by legitimate kingship is restored by the dual influences of Malcolm and Macduff, whose freedom from feminine influences is emphasised by Malcom's virginity, being one 'unknown to woman', and

Macduff's caesarean birth that fulfils the witches' prophecy regarding 'none of woman born'.

As the critic Nicolas Tredell argues, 'the conclusion of the play leaves intact a structure of values in which the masculine principle dominates the feminine. All that is restored is the division which prevailed at the beginning'.[11] However, perhaps by using the end of the play to restore the original, yet divisive system of patriarchal rule that existed at the start of the play, Shakespeare is ultimately warning his audience against the narrow and restrictive definitions of both masculinity and femininity that existed within his culture and which wreaked so much damage.

---

[11] Tredell, *Macbeth* p. 97.

Shakespeare's language

In the 1930s a literary academic, Caroline Spurgeon, wrote a hugely influential critical study of Shakespeare's language, called, somewhat unimaginatively perhaps, Shakes*peare's Imagery and What it Tells Us*. The central idea of Spurgeon's study was that Shakespeare's figurative imagery falls into groups or clusters and these clusters vary from play to play. Moreover, Spurgeon opined that these image clusters are the most important generators of the distinct mood and atmosphere of each play and also convey key thematic concerns. For instance, we might quickly think of the multiple images of animals in *Macbeth*; indeed, like *King Lear*, the Scottish play houses a teeming 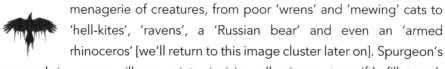 menagerie of creatures, from poor 'wrens' and 'mewing' cats to 'hell-kites', 'ravens', a 'Russian bear' and even an 'armed rhinoceros' [we'll return to this image cluster later on]. Spurgeon's approach is, as you will appreciate, incisive, allowing us to swiftly fillet each play for the seemingly richest cuts of language.

However, since the 1930s Spurgeon's approach has been criticized and refined in various ways. There are three main criticisms: As a pioneering female literary academic writing in the 1930s Spurgeon was constrained by decorum; hence she entirely ignored imagery to do with sex. Critics have also contested her choices of the supposedly dominant image clusters in each play, suggesting alternative clusters that are just as, or even more, significant. Other critics have gone a step further, disagreeing with the privileging of imagery above other features. Why, for instance, is imagery more significant than repeated single words [think of the importance of 'blood' and 'double' in *Macbeth* or how the word 'tyrant' appears fifteen times in the final acts] or other literary devices such as antithesis ['fair is foul and foul is fair']? What about the use of verse, and prose, and Shakespeare's bending and meshing of iambic pentameter with syntax? Aren't characters also pretty important, especially in a text that is written to be performed by actors on a stage? Words, of course, matter, but there's an old cliché that actions speak louder. Surely what characters do is more important than what they say. And so on. No doubt there's even a literary academic out there somewhere who'd argue that the real key to unlocking Shakespeare's plays is his use of prepositions or commas.

Though it might have some limitations, examining the image clusters in any of Shakespeare's plays is still a very useful, productive exercise.

Image clusters in *Macbeth*

i.   Appearance versus reality

Right from the first scene of the play Shakespeare establishes the idea that in this story it's going to be difficult for anyone to distinguish between what is real from what is fake, disguised or fantastical. Not only is goodness going to be mixed up with, and indistinguishable from, evil, but the medium we perceive through, the air itself, is also going to be polluted:

'Fair is foul, and foul is fair:
Hover through the fog and filthy air'.

If there's one overarching theme that links Shakespeare's plays, probably this is it. Indeed, scholars agree that it wasn't only Shakespeare who was obsessed with the theme of appearance versus reality, but that this was one of the dominant thematic preoccupations for all early modern playwrights. Why? Probably because theatre itself was still a new, developing form in Elizabethan England and deliberate confusion between what is real and what is pretence is integral to the nature of theatre itself. After all, the name we give to this art form, a 'play', indicates that it is fundamentally concerned with pretence. When we watch a play, we know that actors are pretending to be real people, that the stage is a pretend version of the real world and so forth. In fact, more than that, we allow ourselves, in the poet Coleridge's phrase to 'suspend our disbelief', and so become active and willing participants in the dramatic illusion. Often this fascination with theatre leads to a sub-set of images drawn from drama and acting running through plays, such as Macbeth's weary observation that life is a 'poor player / That struts and frets his hour upon the stage'. In addition, the interrogation of the power of theatre manifested itself in plays within plays, most famously 'The Mouse-Trap' in *Hamlet*.

Multiple characters in *Macbeth* struggle to distinguish what is real. In this interaction with the Witches, Banquo, for example, labours hard to determine whether they are 'fantastical' or actual 'inhabitants o' the earth'. He is not even certain whether they are alive and human or whether they are merely 'bubbles' of the earth. Nor can he tell whether the Witches are male or female. Meanwhile Macbeth struggles with the ethical implications of the Witches' prophecy, but is unable to work out what is 'ill' from what might be 'good'.

What people say and what they do can be very different. The same is true of Shakespeare's characters. Even when dealing with other humans, humans that they know well, characters in *Macbeth* are easily mislead in their perceptions and misplace their trust. Duncan, for instance, apprised of the Thane of Cawdor's betrayal, may reflect sagely that 'There's no art / To find the mind's construction in the face', but he then entirely trusts the new Thane of Cawdor, Macbeth, and his wife, whom he calls a 'fair and noble hostess'.

If it is hard enough for characters in *Macbeth* to distinguish between what is real from what is not in ordinary circumstances, then how much more difficult will this become when some characters start to deliberately put on disguises to cover their true intentions? Prompted by the Witches' prophecy and by Duncan's announcement that his son, Malcolm, will succeed him as the next King of Scotland, Macbeth tells himself to 'hide' his 'fires', so that the 'light' will not see his 'dark and deep desires'. However, his ability to counterfeit is

 almost immediately questioned by his wife who tells him his face is like an open-book where men 'may read strange matters'. Hence she instructs him to 'look like the innocent flower / But be the serpent under't', an instruction he takes to heart - 'away, and mock the time with fairest show / False face must hide what the false heart doth know'. Characters' ability to read what is really happening and distinguish what is fair from what is foul is also going to be deliberately impaired: echoing the Witches, Lady Macbeth, for example, calls up the power of darkness, 'thick night' to aid her murderous enterprise and obscure her true intentions.

And what if it becomes impossible to distinguish between what is real from what is imagined? What if there is an even more fundamental problem in determining the real material world from things conjured up by the 'heat-oppressed brain'? Macbeth and his wife might be shrewder readers of people then the innocent, trusting Duncan, but once their murder plot has been hatched, both increasingly become ensnared in what philosophers might label an ontological[12] crisis: Macbeth hallucinates a 'dagger' in the air before him as he hurries to kill commit regicide; when he examines his hands after the murder they seem to be covered in so much blood that they are impossible to clean; unlike the rest of his guests, Macbeth sees the ghost of Banquo, while his wife calls this 'the very painting of your fear'; Lady Macbeth herself ends the play in an in-between dreaming-and-waking state, trying to wash an invisible 'damned spot' from her hands and in his final despair, her husband concludes that 'life's but a walking shadow'.

Another cluster of images expresses the appearance and reality theme in terms of clothing and costumes. When told he will become the new Thane of Cawdor, Macbeth asks why he is being dressed in 'borrowed clothes'. A little later, when he resolves not to commit the murder, Macbeth refers to 'wearing' the king's 'golden opinions' to which his wife scornfully replies that has 'dressed himself' in false hopes. Expressing concern about Macbeth's coronation, Macduff worries that his 'old robes' might have been more comfortable than 'our new'. When Macbeth begins to lose his grip on power, this is also expressed using clothing imagery. In Act V Scene 2 Caithness comments that Macbeth 'cannot buckle his distempered cause / Within his belt of rule', while Ross opines that Macbeth feels his title 'Hang loose about him, like a giant's robe / Upon a dwarfish thief'.

And there's another way in which appearance and reality become confused in the play. The doubling language in the play, which we'll consider later, often generates two possible meanings - what the words appear to mean and what they really mean. The Witches' prophecies are, of course, the prime examples.

---

[12] Ontology is the study of the nature of being and of reality.

ii. Animals, monsters and the supernatural

More akin to a tropical jungle than Scotland, the world of *Macbeth* teems with dangerous animals. Mostly these creatures fall into three categories:

- aggressive and/or predatory, with sharp teeth and claws, such as wolves, tigers and bears, or heavily armoured, like rhinos
- associated with darkness, death and/or evil, such as ravens, owls, crows and vultures
- poisonous and also associated with evil, e.g. serpents, snakes and scorpions.

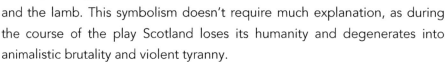

Cowering from these fierce creatures are other smaller, less aggressive animals, such as the wren and the lamb. This symbolism doesn't require much explanation, as during the course of the play Scotland loses its humanity and degenerates into animalistic brutality and violent tyranny.

There seems to be a continuum in Shakespeare's imagery, charting this moral decline. The first stage is humans starting to behave like wild animals: Driven by instinct and lust for power or blood, rather than by reason and principle, humans become natural monsters. As they descend lower, they become less recognisably like fierce creatures from nature and become, instead, unnatural creatures. Finally, humans are transformed into the stuff of nightmares, morphing into supernaturalised creatures – devils, witches, fiends. For instance, once she has called evil spirits to unsex herself, Lady Macbeth, in effect, becomes unnatural, almost a fourth witch. Once apprised of the extent of Macbeth's tyranny, Macduff claims that there is no 'devil' in 'horrid hell', 'more damned / In evils' than Macbeth. Combining the natural with the supernatural, Macduff also calls him a 'hell-kite' and 'hell-hound'. At the end of the play, Malcolm labels Macbeth as 'devilish' and a 'dead butcher', and his wife he calls 'fiend-like'.

Indeed, the word 'natural', in Shakespeare's plays, often operates as a synonym for morally good and wholesome. The night of Duncan's murder, nature was thrown into violent disorder. The old man in Act II Scene 2, embodying wisdom, comments how the darkness now obscuring the 'living light' of day is 'unnatural / Even like the deed that's done', i.e. Duncan's murder. In the same scene, Ross expresses scepticism about the blame falling on Malcolm and Donalbain in terms of what's natural, ''Gainst nature still'. In this light, Lady Macduff's comment that in abandoning her and her son, her husband 'wants the natural touch' raises major doubts about Macduff's character. And the doctor makes a link between Lady Macbeth's sleepwalking and the crimes committed by the Macbeths: 'Unnatural deeds / Do breed unnatural troubles', a phrase that resonates horribly for Macbeth too.

iii.   Sickness and health

Interestingly, by Act V both the invading army and Macbeth understand that Scotland has become diseased and both seek a cure. Caithness describes the assembled invaders as 'the medicine' needed to 'purge' the 'sickly weal' while in the following scene Macbeth discusses a more local infection, asking the doctor whether he can 'minister to a mind diseased' and with 'some sweet, oblivious antidote' cure its troubles. Ostensibly Macbeth is talking here of his wife, but the Doctor picks up the unsubtle subtext, saying that the patient must 'minister to himself'. Macbeth's mind then moves swiftly from the personal to the national:

'If thou couldst, doctor, cast
The water of my land, find her disease,
And purge it to a sound and pristine health…'

The difference, of course, is that the invaders see themselves as the cure and can take action to purge Scotland. In contrast, though we may get the sense that deep-down Macbeth knows where the sickness that blights his country lies, on the surface he is simply casting about for some sort of magical weapon which could 'scour these English hence'.

Unable to provide this weapon and perhaps unwilling to suggest what a proper cure might entail, at the first opportunity the doctor makes a sharp and obviously symbolically resonant exit from Dunsinane. This is the same doctor whose earlier comment about Lady Macbeth's sleepwalking made explicit the symbolic link between disease and immorality in the play. Again, admitting his inability to effect a cure, the doctor says, 'more needs she the divine than the physician'.

Of course, the Witches spread the infection through Scotland's air at the start of the play and conjure it in their chants and potions. They are the source of the sickness. But Lady Macbeth and her husband also consciously call up the forces of darkness and moral infection and spread it further. In murdering Duncan they also murder their own moral health, symbolized by their inability to sleep. Sleep is nature's curative, but, as Lady Macbeth says of her husband he lacks 'the season of all natures, sleep'.

If the Witches and the Macbeths are sources of disease, at least from the point of view of their enemies, then the English king, Edward the Confessor is the  opposite. Aligned with the Scottish rebels seeking to overthrow Macbeth, Edward is the character most associated with medicinal virtues. 'At his touch,' a different doctor tells us, a 'crew of wretched souls' whose illness has defeated medical expertise 'presently amend'. If any sleepy members of the audience hadn't picked up the idea that Edward has the power of good magic to counter the malign magic of the Witches, then the following lines hit them over the head with it; the affliction these poor souls suffer is 'called the evil'.

Like the damned spot Lady Macbeth cannot rub from her hands, the signs of sickness in Scotland make palpable the moral corruption at the heart of the Macbeth's reign. And Edward embodies the 'miraculous' cure. Noticeably in a play whose reference points erstwhile have predominantly been pagan [e.g. 'Bellona's bridegroom', Hecate and Tarquin] the English king is presented in distinctly Christian terms. Spending his time in 'holy prayers', living in 'grace' he offers 'benediction'. He is also not the subject of prophecy, like Macbeth, but has, instead, the 'gift' of it, like the Witches. However, only Edwards's gift for prophecy is 'heavenly'.

iv.   Darkness and light

As we have discussed already, for most of its duration the world of the play is benighted. As with sickness, the primary sources of the darkness appear to be the Witches and the Macbeths. Gathering at night, the Witches are 'the instruments of darkness', 'black and midnight hags' – i.e. embodiments of the dark - while both Macbeths invite the forces of darkness to help them perform their deeds of 'dreadful note'; Lady Macbeth's 'come thick night' is echoed later by her husband's 'come, seeling night'. Duncan's murder in itself seems to generate darkness or shuts out light. After the regicide, even when the new day dawns in Dunsinane, the sky remains unnaturally and ominously dark.

While the Macbeths evoke darkness and night to cover their dark deeds, the exposure of day and light is, of course, associated with the opposite forces of goodness and truth. When Macbeth first learns of Malcolm's succession, he hopes that the 'light' will not 'see his black and deep desires' and when he plans the murder he wishes to conceal it from the 'tender eye' of 'pitiful day'. Whiteness is also associated with innocence, as Lady Macbeth acknowledges when she upbraids her husband after the murder, 'My hands are of your colour; but I shame / To wear a heart so white'. It isn't until Act IV, however, that light really starts to enter the play. Malcolm, for instance, concludes Scene 3 by saying 'the night is long that never finds the day' and in the following scene Lady Macbeth, desperately trying to escape her inner darkness, carries a candle, a flickering, inconstant light. The brightest daylight is 'golden', an adjective in the play that is reserved for the two saintly kings, Duncan and Edward.

Other linguistic devices

Repetition

Many critics have noted the pervasiveness of duplication in *Macbeth*. In terms of characters, for instance, there are two disloyal thanes of Cawdor [Macbeth being the second]; two victorious generals, Banquo and Macbeth; Duncan has two sons and there are two revengers, Malcolm and Macduff. The double pattern runs like a thread through the play's language too. Famously, or perhaps notoriously, the Witches use doubling language in at least three different ways. As we'll discuss when we consider ambiguity and equivocation, and as Macbeth in particular learns too late, their words often carry two meanings, a surface and a hidden one. The three Witches also often repeat words and images in patterns of twos and threes. Think of the first scene: In addition to the fundamental, polluting, 'fair is foul, and foul is fair', the battle is 'lost and won', two familiars are summoned - 'Graymalkin' and 'Paddock' - and the confusion they release will hover through the 'fog and filthy air'. And, of course, the Witches also use the word 'double' itself, doubly so, in fact, in their 'double, double' incantation.

Though they may be the source of the doubling language, the Witches are not alone in using it. As well as more subtler examples of language being double-edged in the play or repeated in double patterns, there are obvious ones where characters use the word 'double' itself: Macbeth and Banquo are described as raining down 'doubly redoubled strokes upon the foe'; Lady Macbeth greets Duncan's entrance to her castle by exclaiming 'All our service/ in every point twice done, and then done double' ; when deciding against the murder of Duncan Macbeth reflects that the King should be protected at Dunsinane by a 'double trust'; Macbeth wishes to doublecheck what the Witches tell him, to 'make assurance double sure' and later he realises how they had spoken to him in a duplicitous 'double sense'.

Other examples of doubling language include 'what's done is done', itself a phrase which is doubled later, with a slight but significant modulation, in 'what's done cannot be undone'. As we have seen, the imagery of the play is also riddled with doubling. Characters frequently put on disguises to hide their thoughts or actions, pretending to be like innocent flowers when really they are snakes in the grass. Antithesis, a device constructed of binaries, such as 'lost and won', 'fair and foul' and 'done/undone', also runs through the play, as we shall go on to explore.

All this doubling feeds into the central overarching theme of the difficulty of distinguishing between appearance and reality. But, as Laurie Maguire points out and we'll explore particularly in our essay on Banquo, it also has a further significant resonance. Although the play is 'populated with parents and children… Banquo has a son, as does Siward, Duncan has two… one entity in the play fails to duplicate or reproduce: the Macbeths themselves'.[13]

And yet. In some ways, doesn't Macbeth create a double of himself, at least from time to time? For instance, once the thought of kingship enters his mind, he splits himself into different public and private selves. Or think of how Macbeth describes himself in the 'is this a dagger' soliloquy. Picturing himself as a separate entity, 'withered Murder', he shifts into the second person, as if dividing himself into two parts, one carrying out the action, the other detached and observing. The figure of 'Murder' is 'alarumed by *his* sentinel', moves with '*his* stealthy pace' towards '*his* design' [our italics]. This curious pattern occurs elsewhere in the play, and we might link it to the use of euphemism as a method of avoiding responsibility for one's own actions. Macbeth's self-division - his capacity to step outside, observe and comment on his own actions and mental state - places fundamental division squarely at the heart of Scotland, yet it is also a crucial factor in maintaining the audience's sympathy for a character who becomes such a brutal tyrant.

Antithesis

Antithesis can operate on a micro scale, for example, as juxtaposition, or within a single line [e.g. 'when the battle's lost and won', 'what's done cannot be undone', 'black Macbeth / will seems as pure as snow'] and also on a macro scale, organizing oppositional patterns across a scene or, indeed, over a whole play. For the latter think, for instance, of the image clusters we've already discussed, such as sickness/health, darkness/light and appearance/reality. In terms of ethics, these antitheses imply that there might a good side against a bad one. But Shakespeare's dramatic method is more complex and nuanced than this. At the heart of all drama is the 'agon', or conflict, and Shakespeare is particularly adept at presenting this conflict from different sides and perspectives, without biasing one side above the other. His grammar school education had trained him in 'in utramque partem', the ability to argue both sides of a question. So, for instance, in *Macbeth* we

---

[13] Maguire, *Studying Shakespeare*, p.203.

condemn, but also sympathise with, or at least can understand, the Macbeths, while, on the other hand, niggling questions undermine our willingness to side with his rivals: Banquo [why doesn't he expose Macbeth's crime when he has the chance? Does self-interest trump his loyalty to Duncan?], Macduff [didn't he abandon his family? Isn't he prepared to have a sinful king rule Scotland?] and Malcolm [Is he a coward? Does he exploit Macduff? Is he manipulative and perhaps untrustworthy?].

Characteristically Shakespeare sets up apparent opposites and then, over the course of a play's action blurs the dividing lines. In *Macbeth* this blurring happens at the very start of the play when the Witches chant, 'fair is foul, and foul is fair'. Here we have an antithesis, foul/fair, but our ability to distinguish between the two, a pretty fundamental distinction in life, is going to be deliberately impeded.

Euphemism, ambiguity and equivocation

As the aptly named academic Russ MacDonald puts it, *Macbeth* is a play chock-full with dangerously unreliable, unstable language, 'double talk, slithery language, wicked persuasion, lies.'[14] As we've noted, the main sources of the doubling language in the play are the Macbeths and the Witches. While the weird sisters use ambiguous and equivocal language to tempt and eventually trick Macbeth, Macbeth and his wife use euphemistic and equivocal language, especially when thinking about their darkest deeds.

In a brilliant and detailed discussion of Macbeth's 'If it were done' speech, Simon Palfrey comments that 'to peep behind the blanket of euphemism is to see true terror'[15]. Consider how Macbeth avoids using the word 'murder' in this soliloquy, hiding it behind the blanket of both the pronoun 'it' and the verb 'done':

'If it were done, when 'tis done, then 'twere well /

---

[14] MacDonald, *The Language of Tragedy*, in *The Cambridge Companion to Shakespearian Tragedy*, p.46.

[15] Palfrey, *Doing Shakespeare*, p.69.

It were done quickly.'

Three times in quick succession Macbeth imagines 'it' being 'done', but he also avoids properly imagining the act by leaving it unnamed. Palfrey notes how, as Macbeth turns over the thought in his mind, he even skims nervously over the word 'it', subsuming it into ''tis' and ''twere'. And working with the euphemistic language there's also ambiguity here. Take the phrase 'when 'tis done'. This could refer to two different moments in time, during the action itself – when it is being done - but also to afterwards, looking back on the action – when it has been done. Furthermore, this temporally uncertain phrase hangs in the middle of a line that otherwise would be far more decisive. Similarly, even when she is alone, waiting for her husband to return after killing Duncan, even when no-one else can hear her, Lady Macbeth also shies away from using the words 'kill' and 'murder'. Macbeth is 'about it' she says and adds that she would have 'done 't', if the sleeping king had not looked like her father. Even when the Macbeths discuss the murder in private between themselves, they continually use euphemistic expressions, saying Duncan must be 'provided for', calling the killing variously the 'great business', 'this business' and the 'enterprise'. Perhaps there is an additional reason for this coded, euphemistic language. Perhaps Macbeth and Lady Macbeth avoid naming the act of murder because, consciously or subconsciously, they fear being overhead, exposed and held to account.

The best example of the Witches' doubling, equivocal language is, of course, the prophecies that they make to Macbeth. In particular, the language in the prophecy that 'Macbeth shall never vanquished be, until / Great Birnam wood to high Dunsinane hill / Shall come against him' pulls semantically into two different directions, allowing two possible, contradictory interpretations. On the one hand, as Macbeth takes it, these words seem to mean that he is safe. But, as we discover, there's enough semantic wriggle room in the words to still have been true even when the opposite happens. After all, the temporal word 'until' indicates that Macbeth's safety will only be temporary, and the same confident verb 'shall' is used both about Macbeth's security and about the wood's moving.

The porter in Act II Scene 3 talks explicitly about and comically riffs on the theme of equivocation. He suggests that, although, equivocating may be profitable on earth, those who can 'swear in both the scale against either scale' won't be able to 'equivocate to heaven' [probably referencing the notorious contemporary trial of the Jesuit priest, Father Garnet]. The porter jokes that 'drink may be said to be an equivocator with lechery' because it has two contradictory effects; it 'makes him and it mars him'. The porter's lewd, humorous comments resonate with the themes of ambition and temptation. Like drink, lust for power, 'makes' Macbeth, but also 'mars' him, 'sets him on' his course of action, but also 'takes him off', 'equivocates him in a sleep' and, finally, when he learns that he is not in fact safe from Macduff gives 'him the lie, leaves him'.

Whereas Banquo is immediately sceptical about trusting the Witches' words, 'oftentimes, to win us to our harm / the instruments of darkness tell us truths / win us with honest trifles, to betray's / In deepest consequence', for Macbeth such insight comes much later. It is not until Act V, when reports come in that Birnam wood appears to be moving towards his castle that Macbeth begins 'to doubt th' equivocation of the fiend'. Confronted soon after in battle by Macduff, when he discovers the equivocal language of 'no man of woman born', Macbeth finally decides that 'these juggling fiends' must be 'no more believed'. A crucial revelation. But for Macbeth it comes far too late.

Words, words, words

Off the top of your head which words, other than function words such as pronouns, conjunctions and prepositions, would you say crop up the most frequently in Macbeth? Here's our quick list: 'Sleep' - 'amen' - 'tyrant' - 'time' - 'blood' - 'man' - 'fear' - 'darkness' - 'double' - 'done'. Some of these words are repeated in high density in a short space of time, notably the first two in our list after the murder of Duncan. Other words are distributed more evenly across the play. As Frank Kermode opines, 'in these echoing words and themes, these repetitions that are so unlike the formal repetitions of an earlier rhetoric, we come close to what were Shakespeare's deepest interests'.[16]

Verse, prose and syntax

Though well-ordered verse is often a linguistic marker of nobility in Shakespeare's plays and although there's a general pattern of verse being given to the high-born or morally noble characters and prose to the lower born or less moral, it would be a mistake to assume that Shakespeare's language always rigidly adheres to this pattern. Hamlet, for instance, frequently speaks in prose. Interestingly, unlike other tragic heroes, Macbeth, however, speaks entirely in verse. We might conclude from this that he must therefore be the most noble of the tragic heroes. If were to do so, we'd be wrong. Because it is not simply the fact of speaking in verse that conveys nobility, it's the distinctive handling of the form that really counts. And, like the ill-fitting clothes of kingship that he so uneasily wears, Macbeth's linguistic struggles emphasise his battle to cover his desires, hide his intentions and finally with performing the role of king.

Simon Palfrey, writing astutely about Macbeth's language comments that 'if the iambic pentameter is often Shakespeare's measure of ease and decorum' then for Macbeth it is often an 'awkward barrier to trip upon or stutter over'.[17] In other words, disorder in metre and syntax are used by Shakespeare to signal disorder within the mind. In particular, as Palfrey outlines, stumbling pauses, half-lines and overlong lines, metrical blips and torturous, tortured syntax, characterise many of Macbeth's often nervy and twitchy utterances. Indeed, the proliferation of these non-fluency features often threatens to break Macbeth's jagged verse down into prose. Hence, as Palfrey puts it, 'the metrical form… is tracing and encasing Macbeth's movements of mind'.

---

[16] Kermode, *Shakespeare's Language*, p.216.

[17] Palfrey, *Doing Shakespeare*, pp.198-203.

The playwright

Had we but the space and time [as well as the skill, the scholarship and, indeed, the inclination] we could, perhaps, provide you, our avid reader, with an exhaustive account of the life and work of the world's most famous writer. After all, the Shakespeare scholar, James Shapiro managed to write a highly engaging account of just one year, albeit a monumentally creative year, in the bard's relatively short life.[18] On the other hand, notoriously, very little information actually exists about Shakespeare's life; famously one of the only extant official documents is his will and its curious instruction to leave his wife his second-best bed. Of course, that gaping biographical vacuum hasn't stopped scholars, biographers and novelists; in fact it's invited them to jump right in and fill it with all sorts of colourful speculations, such as the story that Shakespeare originally fled Stratford because he'd been illegally poaching deer and the preposterous idea that Shakespeare didn't really write his own plays, nor presumably all of his own poems, because he wasn't from the right class.

But, we haven't the space or time for such fanciful speculating [whether we have the other qualities we'll leave you to decide]. So, what can usefully be said about William Shakespeare [1564-1616] in a couple of pages or so? Firstly, that he was a middle-class boy, grammar school educated, and that he

---

[18] Shapiro, *1606, The Year of Lear*.

didn't attend either of the great universities of Oxford or Cambridge. This fact partly accounts for the claim that Shakespeare couldn't have written his plays as, so the argument goes, he had neither the life experiences nor the sophisticated education to do so, a claim unpleasantly whiffing of snobbery. How did a middle-class boy from the provinces write so brilliantly about kings, queens and princes and different times and cultures? Perhaps he read widely, observed keenly and used his prodigious imagination.

Secondly, at the tender age even for the Elizabethans of just eighteen Shakespeare married an older woman, Anne Hathaway, who was twenty-six and already pregnant. This is a point to be borne in mind whenever Shakespeare is writing about disinherited and bitter children, those born out of wedlock and therefore labelled as 'bastards' in his world.

Thirdly, Shakespeare was an actor and many scholars think he probably took roles, albeit relatively minor ones, in his own plays. He was a member of an acting group, called the Lord Chamberlain's Men who had a theatre built to house their performances – the Globe theatre.

Fourthly, Shakespeare was not only a highly successful playwright but also a shrewd businessman. By middle-age he had become wealthy enough to buy the 'second largest' house in Stratford. By this time, his acting company had been promoted up the social ladder to 'The King's Men', with a royal charter and King James I as their patron, and they had purchased a second theatre.

Fifthly, Shakespeare was a highly accomplished poet as well as a playwright. Writing a decent sonnet was considered de rigueur for an Elizabethan courtier. Shakespeare did not write one decent sonnet, of course not, he wrote a sonnet sequence, a bigger and better and more sophisticated sonnet sequence than anyone has managed before or since, arguably. Comprising over a hundred and fifty sonnets, the sequence dramatizes the story of an intense love triangle, involving Shakespeare, a handsome young man and a dark lady.

Sixthly, Shakespeare is absolutely everywhere. He is the only writer whose work by law has to be studied in English schools. His poems and plays are read, studied and performed across the globe, from Australia to China, from India to Zambia, and have been translated into almost every major language, including Klingon[19]. Unsurprisingly, he's the best-selling writer ever. Estimates suggest that there have been over four hundred film version of his plays. Phrases and words Shakespeare coined are used every day by thousands, perhaps millions of people, sometimes consciously and sometimes because they have become an integral part of the fabric of our language. And that's still not the be-all and end-all: His head appears on bank notes, cups and tea-towels and he is a crucial part of the English tourism industry and our national identity. In this country alone, there are several theatre companies dedicated to his work, including a royal one, the RSC. In short, Shakespeare was, and is still, a phenomenon.

Some critics suggest that the boy from Stratford got lucky; his work spread the globe because first the Elizabethans and after them the Victorians explored and conquered much of the globe and everywhere the English went they took Shakespeare along with them. But, even then, that doesn't explain why Shakespeare and not another English writer became so ubiquitous.

Read the best scenes from any of his plays and the best scenes in *Macbeth*, in particular, such as the ones leading up to and after the murder, and you can see for yourself why Shakespeare became such a phenomenon. No, he wasn't a genius at plotting. In fact, famously, Shakespeare lifted the story lines for most of his plays from other works. The sheer brilliance of these scenes comes instead from an extraordinary acuity about what makes humans tick, from the keenest appreciation of how we interact with others in society, including the ways we speak, and from the capacity to render human experiences in the most powerful and vivid language imaginable, while also managing to explore big thematic ideas, ideas that remain endlessly relevant.

---

[19] Apparently 'taH pagh taHbe' is Klingon for the very famous opening to a speech by Hamlet.

Shakespeare's world

The socio-historical contexts to *Macbeth* are closely tied to the succession to the throne of the new king of England in 1603, James I, his beliefs about kingship and witchcraft, and the early years of his reign, particularly the controversy surrounding the Gunpowder Plot of 1605. James I was very interested in the arts and became the patron of Shakespeare's acting company with the company being renamed The King's Men after James' coronation. *Macbeth* was first performed in front of James I at Hampton Court Palace on August 7, 1606, with it even being rumoured Shakespeare played the part of Lady Macbeth. It is therefore unsurprising that Shakespeare would wish to please and flatter the new king and there are numerous references to James' reign and beliefs throughout the play.

The decision to write a play about a Scottish King was no doubt influenced by the fact James had ruled as King of Scotland from 1567 until being made king of both nations in 1603. Shakespeare used the historical work, Holinshed's Chronicles [1577] as his source material for the play, but made a number of changes to the historical account, partly for dramatic purposes, but also to please James. Shakespeare changed Duncan from the selfish and ineffectual leader he is portrayed as in Holinshed to a kindly and respected ruler, probably to emphasise the evil of regicide. According to Holinshed, Macbeth killed Duncan in battle for circumventing Macbeth's legitimate claim to the throne and then ruled Scotland for seventeen years before becoming a tyrant and eventually being killed. Shakespeare turns Macbeth into a cowardly murderer and shows his fall into despotism as immediate, again to demonstrate the catastrophic consequences that follow the usurpation of a king. And while Banquo is presented as a duplicitous character who plots with Macbeth against Duncan in Holinshed, Shakespeare makes him a noble, loyal and idealised figure who plays no part in the murder.

More significant than the changes Shakespeare makes to his source material is the way he engages in contemporary debates about kingship, especially those expressed by James I in the two books he wrote on the subject, *The True Law of Free Monarchies* [1598] and *Basilikon Doron* [1599]. In both works, James set forth his arguments supporting the doctrine of the *Divine Right of Kings*, the belief that God chooses the kings of nations to rule as his representatives on earth. Hence to rebel against a king or, even worse, to attempt to kill them, is a direct act of mutiny against God. In *Macbeth*, Shakespeare appears to give his support to such beliefs, particularly in the way Duncan is presented as God's divinely-appointed ruler whose 'virtues will plead like angels' against the act of regicide.

Belief in the Divine Right of Kings was supported by the medieval concept of the *Great Chain of Being*, a hierarchical model of the universe which placed God at the top of existence, followed by angels, then humans, animals, plants and finally minerals. Each category was subdivided into order of importance. Among humans the King was ranked at the top in order of importance, followed by Lords and noblemen, merchants and so on downwards to peasants. Everything in creation had its specific place in the hierarchy according to God's perfect will, so that any disruption to the Great Chain would lead to chaos and disorder. This is why, following the murder of Duncan, strange unnatural occurrences start to happen in the natural world, such as the owl killing a falcon or Duncan's horses eating each other as mentioned in Act II Scene Four; a disruption to one part of the hierarchy reverberates through the whole chain. Only when the usurper Macbeth is killed and Malcolm, the legitimate and rightful heir to Duncan is crowned, can order and health be restored to the sick and suffering nation of Scotland.

Shakespeare's stark warnings against the catastrophic consequences of regicide in *Macbeth* are, of course, closely related to the defining event of James I early reign - the discovery of the *Gunpowder Plot* in 1605 where

Catholic conspirators planned to assassinate the new king by blowing up the houses of Parliament. The plotters, including Guy Fawkes whose job was to detonate the dynamite and Robert Catesby, the ringleader, were angered by continued persecution of Catholics under James I and hoped to kill him and replace him with a Catholic King. Shakespeare makes many references to the Gunpowder Plot in the play, such as allusions to equivocation made by the porter and Macbeth that refer to the Jesuit Priest, Henry Garnet, who tried to hide his awareness of the plot through the practice of equivocation - using language in an ambiguous way so as to disguise the truth without technically lying. As we have already mentioned, Garnet had become infamous among the public as 'the great equivocator'. Lady Macbeth's counsel to Macbeth to 'look like th'innocent flower, / But be the serpent under't' also refers to a medal of a serpent hiding among flowers made to commemorate the thwarting of the plot. As well as specific references to the Gunpowder Plot, the whole theme of the play seems to be a warning against regicide by demonstrating its evil consequences to individuals and the nation as a whole, a message that would have undoubtedly been well received by James. Some commentators even suggest Shakespeare wrote *Macbeth* to convince James he wasn't involved in the plot himself, as he shared personal links to some of the conspirators and might have been worried about falling under suspicion.

The many references to witchcraft in the play would also have greatly appealed to the new king, who had himself written a treatise on witchcraft titled *Daemonologie* [1597]. James believed that as King and God's chosen representative on earth, he was particularly susceptible to attack from the Devil. He blamed a storm at sea that nearly sunk a ship he was travelling on in 1589 on witches that he believed had conjured the storm to kill him. When he returned to shore James ordered a witch hunt in Berwick that resulted in seventy women being accused of witchcraft, many of whom were arrested, tortured and even executed. In *Macbeth*, Shakespeare presents the Witches as forces of evil that manipulate Macbeth in order to disrupt God's order and bring disorder and chaos to Scotland. However, the Witches' power is limited and temporary; they do not take any direct action in the play and only prophesy what has been destined to take place. Their deceiving of Macbeth through their equivocations show how the forces of evil cannot be trusted and ultimately, goodness and order are restored to Scotland when Malcolm is crowned king. Or so it seems.

The depiction of the Witches in the play, who were seen as corrupting influences of a malign femininity, reflects the subordinate position of women within the patriarchal structures of Jacobean society. The activities associated with witchcraft, such as flying on broomsticks that were meant to be used for cleaning, or making potions in cauldrons that should have been used for cooking, suggests how witches came to symbolize a threatening subversion of gender roles and independence from male control, something also hinted at in Banquo's reaction to the Witches that 'you should be women, / And yet your beards forbid me to interpret / That you are so.' In contrast, women within Jacobean society were expected to be dutiful wives and mothers, obedient to their husbands and nurturing of their children. They enjoyed very few legal rights, received little education and were viewed as property to be passed from father to husband. This is why Lady Macbeth's manipulation of her husband and corrupted maternality expressed in lines such as 'take my milk for gall' and 'dashed the brains out' would have been so shocking to Shakespeare's audience as it completely reverses the ways in which women were expected to behave. While it is tempting to read the play as a confirmation of the misogynistic attitudes towards women - Lady Macbeth's attempts to control her husband misfire and she eventually kills herself - we could also read the play as a challenge to the patriarchal power structures from which women in Shakespeare's day were excluded. Perhaps if women had been granted more equality, Lady Macbeth would not have needed to take the drastic measures she did.

Critical commentaries on key scenes

Act One

Anticipating the cross-cutting techniques of film directors, in Act I Shakespeare swiftly switches between very different perspectives, from the Witches on a blasted heath to the Scottish King, Duncan, and his retinue to Macbeth and Banquo travelling back after battle. Famously from the outset the Witches inform us that nothing will be as it seems in this play and, worse, that sometimes 'fair' will appear 'foul' and vice versa. A modern film director might be tempted to add a scene that Shakespeare only reports, that of the brutal battle between the Scots and the invading Norwegians. Clearly it would have been challenging [and expensive] for the Globe stage and its actors to produce a convincing full-blown clash between large armies, so there are practical reasons why Shakespeare made this choice. But does the playwright gain anything by having the battle reported by witnesses?

Certainly Shakespeare makes both the Captain and Ross highly articulate witnesses, able to describe the violent action in bold and colourful strokes. The Captain's descriptions - of Macbeth's sword ['smoked with bloody execution'] and Macbeth 'Like Valour's minion' - culminate in the horribly vivid depiction of the evisceration of the traitor Macdonald: 'he unseamed him from the nave to th' chops', a rather difficult action to portray well on stage. While the Captain's information appears to cast Macbeth in a heroic light, the audience will be both cognisant of his extreme violence and remember the Witches' claim in the previous scene about appearances being deceptive. To underline the point, Shakespeare has the Captain echo the doubling language of Witches, 'with double tracks / so they doubly redoubled'. So, reporting the battle rather than staging it allows Shakespeare to generate anticipation in the audience and set up expectations about Macbeth as a character.

Rather than go through Act I scene by scene we're going to focus attention on a key scene, Scene 7. However, before exploring that scene in detail a quick summary of the action up until that point will be useful: Having defeated the invading Norwegians, returning from battle Macbeth and Banquo chance upon the Witches and hear their prophecies. Again the Witches' language is echoed, here in Macbeth's first words in the play. Some of the Witches' predictions come immediately true as Macbeth and Banquo are rewarded by Duncan for their heroic endeavours. Soon afterwards Macbeth writes home to his wife, informing her that he is predicted to become king and she resolves to aid him in achieving this as swiftly as possible. Together they hatch a plan to commit the sin of regicide - to murder the innocent Duncan, who, oblivious to the danger, has come to their castle to celebrate the recent victories.

Act I Scene 7 is the second time we have witnessed the Macbeths conspiring in secret together in their private chamber. The scene begins with a soliloquy [discussed in detail in another part of this guide] in which Macbeth determines against the murder. In the rest of the scene, only around fifty lines or so, Lady Macbeth sets about changing his mind back again. This is the crux of Act I; the whole future shape of the play depends on the electric exchange depicted in this scene. For a few intense minutes, things are absolutely on a knife's edge: if Macbeth had had a bit more about him and his wife a bit less, then the murder of Duncan would never have happened.

Frequently in his plays, Shakespeare alternates between public and private scenes, facilitating dramatic evocation of the fundamental theme of the differences between appearances and reality. In the preceding scene, for example, Lady Macbeth had appeared to graciously welcome Duncan – the man she will help her husband to murder – to Dunsinane. In Scene 7 we see what's really going on behind the mask of appearances, both in Macbeth's mind and within the couple's relationship.

Macbeth's introspective musings are interrupted by his more practically-minded wife. Doubts about Macbeth's ability to perform his new treacherous role are multiplying, for the audience and for Lady Macbeth: Firstly, he seems entirely lost in his thoughts; secondly, guiltily, he seems to be avoiding Duncan's company – he was absent from the previous scene when as host he'd have been expected to welcome his royal guests and now he's left the banquet early while the guests are still eating. Thirdly, he doesn't appear to have a grip on events, let alone a command of them, relying on his wife to keep him informed - 'what news?', 'hath he asked for us?' From the moment Lady Macbeth enters, the pace of the scene accelerates rapidly, with a tense, staccato back-and-forth between husband and wife.

The lines are chockful with questions. Who asks them, how they ask them, who answers and how they answer are fundamental indicators of the shifting power dynamic between the Macbeths and, along with the fact that she speaks far more than her husband, the questions emphasise Lady Macbeth's overall dominance of this critical exchange. For instance, she answers her husband's first question in brief, cursory terms, just four words, before she fires a far sharper question back at him. Her question is barbed, with an accusatory tone: 'Why have you left the chamber?' Cleary, she is upbraiding him for scanting his duties as host. When he asks another neutral, information-seeking question she responds with a withering counter-question, the sense that she shoots this back at him implied by the way she completes his line.

Attempting to assert himself, Macbeth ignores this question. He employs the first-person plural pronoun, wrapping his wife's actions in his own, and the modal verb, 'will' in a declarative line that is meant to resound with authority:

'We will proceed no further in this business'.

Though he goes on to justify himself in measured terms, any persuasive effect is diluted: He feels he has to explain and qualify a decision he has made on both their accounts.

If you were the director of this scene how might you instruct your actors to speak? It's a conspiratorial scene, where dark deeds are imagined and planned, so perhaps the actors should be speaking in whispers and quickly to convey the tense mixture of excitement and dread. How would you play the lines above? Where, for instance, are the Macbeths standing in relation to each other? Where do they look? Does Macbeth perhaps pull away from his wife as he says the murder will not go ahead? Does he maybe avoid eye contact? When she responds with her probing, insulting, provocative volley of questions does she perhaps move towards him, compel him to look at her, even grab him by the shoulders?

Any hopes Macbeth had of settling the matter are blown to smithereens by his wife's bitter, excoriating response. Again she completes his line, 'Was the hope drunk?' She shoots two scornful questions at him in quick succession and follows these up with some heavy-hitting emotional blackmail.

 Straightaway two more fierce questions fly at him. Notice how she leaves no space at all for him to refute any of her accusations. Each of her questions demeans, shames and belittles Macbeth, striking at his core sense of self, his masculine pride: She questions whether he is really in control of himself ['drunk']; whether he is sincere and committed, or only superficial, ['dressed']; whether he is healthy or diseased ['green and pale']; she implies that he's frightened ['afeard'] and that his desires are braver than his actions; she implies that really he's a 'coward' and that he's also a ridiculous figure, foolish and feminised ['like the poor cat'] to be pitied or laughed at. Clearly, she knows him well and her verbal arrows are well aimed.

By now, the conversation is almost crackling with tension. His reply, 'Pry'thee peace' completes her last line - a desperate, defensive interruption to try to stop the barrage. How do you imagine an actor saying this line? Perhaps he raises his voice, shouts it, accompanied by a demonstrative gesture of some sort. Nevertheless, it is only a plea and actually signals weakness rather than strength. Once again Macbeth tries to sound firm and resolute, ending with a terse, monosyllabic line whose sense is emphasised by its regular metre, 'who **dares** do **more** is **none**'. But it's not strong enough. Her barrage has only paused, not stopped, a pause that allowed him to lift his head above the parapet. Again she retorts immediately, completing a line he might have hoped would have resonated for a moment or two at least. Derisively she spits back at him, 'What beast was't then?'

What follows is not, however, merely an emotional diatribe, a letting rip at Macbeth's vacillation. A steely logic begins to come into play, lambasting, but also persuading at the same time. From scorn, she switches adeptly to flattery. If he were to carry out the murder, he would be 'so much more the man'. In addition, she points out the time is ripe, the moment opportune, and then comes her final coup-de-grace. It's an extraordinary few lines in which she weighs her determination against his, and finds his wanting. Lady Macbeth imagines killing her own child, straight after performing the most loving and motherly of tasks. Moreover, she imagines doing this while the baby is still 'smiling' and imagines the killing in the most brutally visceral terms, 'dash'd the brains out'. Does she mean it? Or is this just the crescendo to a wave of rhetoric? The audience must be appalled, but Macbeth is persuaded, offering, only a daunted and tentative question, a question that is, in an already now familiar pattern, immediately pounced upon by his wife.

Her tone is incredulous, the words abrupt, a verbal punch perhaps – 'we fail?' Superficially it's another question, but it doesn't require him to answer. She will answer her own question. An imperative, 'screw your courage to the sticking place' and then the logical planning comes out; a plan – drug the guards, kill Duncan, blame them. Yet more rhetorical questions follow, engaging him, but also cutting him out of any decision-making. Macbeth cannot turn this rhetorical tide. Impressed, daunted by his wife, swept away by her words, he can only offer a final question. It's less direct and the voltage is much lower than any of hers. Meekly, he seeks her assurance, 'Will it not be received…?' In contrast, she answers with yet another counter-question, one that lands like a challenge 'Who dares receive it other…?'

He certainly dare not demur. And so, Macbeth is 'settled'. Taking comfort in imagining the task at hand to be a manly, physical one - 'bend up/ Each corporeal agent to this terrible feat' - he settles to be the brawn to his wife's brains. Ostensibly, Macbeth ending the exchange shows him reasserting himself, recovering power and control. He finishes, for example, with an imperative, 'away', and a jaunty summarising couplet. But really, isn't this just a fig-leaf to cover his hurt male pride? We have the distinct sense that she is allowing him to have the last word. Again, we might wonder what the actress playing Lady Macbeth should do while he speaks these lines. In any case, his final words only reiterate what she has already instructed him to do in their previous meeting, 'To beguile the time / Look like the time'. Nobody's fooled; not him, not her, not the audience. From the moment she entered the room, Lady Macbeth has been in the box-set and driven this whole conversation with her furiously impassioned rhetoric. At this point in the story, clearly, it's Lady Macbeth who wears the trousers in this family.

And Act I ends where it began, with a promise of deception and double-dealing. Echoing the Witches, Macbeth's final line in Scene 7 is 'False face must hide what the false heart doth know'.

Act Two

After the intense action and moral anguish of Act I, Act II of *Macbeth* represents something of a slowing down of the action while simultaneously ratcheting up the emotional intensity. Gone are the Witches, gone are the vivid stories of bloody slaughter and male warrior prestige and gone the shocking, first glimpse of Lady Macbeth's darkest ambitions. Instead the location is predominantly confined to Macbeth's Inverness castle and the time to merely a handful of deadly hours. The night-time setting of Scenes 1 and 2 as well as the murky dawn of Scene 3 symbolically announce Macbeth's descent into evil and the ambiguous uncertainty that follows it. The scenes are very short but packed with import, a combination which creates a terrible dramatic intensity for the audience to endure. This intensity is amplified by the array of noises: bells, knockings, screaming owls, shrieking crickets and the general mayhem of what Macbeth rather underwhelmingly describes as a 'rough night'. This maelstrom and the pathetic fallacy of a great storm symbolises the terrible transgression of natural order unleashed by the Macbeth's regicidal scheming.

Notably, looking at the act as a whole it begins and ends not with Macbeth but two of his greatest soon-to-be foes: Banquo and Macduff. You can add a third if we consider Fleance as future king of Scotland. We are still early enough in the play to allow a certain jostling of characters in the action. In Act II, Banquo, Macduff and Lady Macbeth are still as dramatically important as Macbeth, whereas, once Macbeth gains power, he dwarfs them all in stature with the play essentially becoming a one-man show after Banquo's murder.

Act II still presents a vulnerable Macbeth, with whom the audience can still sympathise, or at least empathise. It is still possible to view him as a decent man and brave soldier operating in politically treacherous times, where Macbeth's terrible ambition seems to be a product of his time rather than an inherent personality trait. Act II is also the last time we see the Macbeths as equals.

Here Lady Macbeth's dynamic darkness, relentless ambition and steely resolve are all at least the equal of Macbeth's manly violence. In fact, Act II can be viewed as Lady Macbeth's zenith in the play – here her feminine scheming, manipulation and sharp tongue are shown as more lethal and effective than Macbeth's expertise in killing. His heavy-handed clumsiness and awkwardness only accentuate her nimble quickness of mind and action. At this point they remain the perfect partners in greatness… but not for much longer. After Act II Macbeth cleaves away from his wife and accelerates his descent into depraved tyranny. This begs a fundamental question: what type of story would we see had they remained close conspirators?

With all tragic heroes there is an engaging agony in contemplating how they could have made different choices and the consequences of alternative actions. Mainly due to its unusually concentrated focus on one plot and one protagonist, *Macbeth* is particularly open to such considerations. Most tragic journeys reveal a key decision that forces the tragic hero's greatness to unravel and the weaving of their demise to begin. With Macbeth surely it must be his decision to murder his king, a man who stays with him 'in double trust' as king, kinsman and guest. However, isn't blaming this decision for Macbeth's downfall a little too simplistic? The most obvious reason against doing so is because it is not really his decision; it's his wife's. If he has been able to disengage his bruised masculine bravado from their discussion, he may have held his nerve and listened to the calm logic that proclaimed that 'we will proceed no further in this business'. Still, it's at best a 50-50 decision. Arguably it's a series of choices that Macbeth makes fully on his own that precipitate his downfall, beginning with the treacherous decision to murder Banquo.

But surely the decision that seals his irreversible peripeteia[20] comes after the comes after the banquet scene in Act III when, with terrifying nihilism and inhumanity, he states: 'I am in blood / Stepped so far, that should I wade no more, / Returning were as tedious as go o'er'. The decision to slaughter the innocent Macduff family and let 'The very firstlings of my heart shall be / The firstlings of my hand' in Act IV is merely an extension of that earlier decision. Macbeth's scorching regret and guilt-ridden trauma in Act II, however, still permit the audience [or some of us] to stick with him for a little longer.

These what-if scenarios haunt the play. Instability and uncertainty is exemplified by sudden lurches in the tone and atmosphere of Act II. Unpredictability is present from the start of the act where Banquo and Fleance's late night conversation at the start of Scene 1 reveals Banquo's sleeplessness, worryingly tormented as he is by vague 'cursed thoughts'. Quickly this gives way to a cagey conversation between Banquo and Macbeth about the Witches' prophecies and, tellingly, Macbeth's request that Banquo stand by him when the time comes [for what exactly is never articulated but Banquo is shrewd enough to guess it will not involve the 'honour' Macbeth suggests]. Obviously, Shakespeare's use of dramatic irony ensures the audience knows that 'honour' has nothing at all to do with what will enfold and the famous dagger soliloquy that follows confirms this. This soliloquy is a condensation of the moral instability that Macbeth has shown previously. The hallucination externalises the internal workings of Macbeth's feverish mind, while the graphic descriptions of 'gouts of blood' on the imaginary dagger emphasise the brutality of what is about to happen. In telling contrast, the Macbeths use euphemistic language, refusing to articulate the words 'murder' or 'kill', seeking to hide behind distancing language, such as 'the bloody business' and 'he is about it'. The soliloquy moves suddenly from the floating dagger to a hellish view of nocturnal life as one full of 'Witchcraft' and 'withered Murder'. Contrasting the extended meditation of the soliloquy 'A bell rings' and Macbeth suddenly runs to perpetrate the much-awaited but nevertheless dreaded regicide.

---

[20] Aristotle's term for a decisive turning point in a play..

Significantly, almost as if it is too unbearable to witness, Shakespeare insists that this taboo action takes place off-stage - a great contrast to the murder of the Macduff family at the end of Act IV, which does take place on stage. The former instance is a clever dramatic strategy, as the audience cannot see the 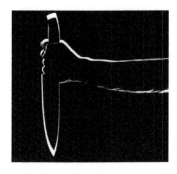 lead-up to the murder, which confers more suspense-filled unpredictability on the play. Secondly it makes us imagine the murder in as gruesome a way as our imaginations allow. Undoubtedly, the latter killing with its explicit murder of innocents in front of the audience both condemns Macbeth's tyrannical reign while also exposing our helplessness [and the ordinary citizen in a tyrannical state] to oppose the evil deeds of powerful men. Perhaps this helplessness to intervene is also part of the power of Duncan's off-stage murder. While Lady Macbeth revels in the 'fire' that drink has given her, we are more concerned with the off-stage events, helpless to stop them, denied even the power of spectating upon the event. Scene 2 at last delivers the climax and aftermath of the much-deliberated decision to murder Duncan. Given Macbeth's personality and his wife's doubts about being 'too full o the milk of human kindness' it is no surprise when he wanders back onstage traumatised and, in most productions, splattered with the reddest blood the props department can find.

The first interaction between the schemers is unsettling and fragmented. Macbeth returns to the stage asking 'Who's there? What ho?' which suggests disorientation, as one would reasonably expect him to know it's his own wife. Whereas in the previous scene he could see things in front of him that weren't there, now he cannot see things that are in front of him: his wife. Nor does she seem to see him either: it takes her six lines before she enquires 'My husband?' How can she not recognise her own husband?! The only way this could be feasible is if he is so traumatised of facial expression or so covered in blood and gore as to be unrecognisable. Of course, there is another explanation: So manic have they both become that they are unrecognisable to each other [him needing the almost altered state of the berserker to complete the deadly deed; and her becoming transformed by drunkenness and possible arousal at the culmination of their scheme]. There is a further option, which would be quite an atmospheric one: the darkening of the stage so that they literally cannot see each other would be both practical, but also symbolic. Either way, they would have to be located on opposite sides of the stage and probably facing away from each other before finding each other - generating a visually shocking clash of bright blood and oppressive dark. Clever costume choices here could combine also to create quite a visually arresting spectacle.

The strange fragments of speech and the several questions that follow their reunion all signify two people on the edge, jumpy and nervous and not thinking straight:

Macbeth: I have done the deed. Didst thou not hear a noise?
Lady Macbeth: I heard the owl scream and the crickets cry.
                    Did not you speak?
Macbeth: When?
Lady Macbeth: Now.
Macbeth: As I descended?
Lady Macbeth: Ay.
Macbeth: Hark, who lies i'the second chamber?

Their subsequent conversation is a microcosm of what went before. Macbeth dominates the dialogue with understandable angst and regret about his actions, his fixation on how he could not say 'Amen' [surely illustrating the regicide as a sacrilegious act, something that Macduff claims in the next scene] and another imagining, the voice that proclaims 'Sleep no more. / Macbeth does murder sleep'. Lady Macbeth's lines are short, almost overwhelmed by the outpouring of emotion from her husband, but sure enough the roles reverse and she re-establishes control. Her former tough love returns as she chastises Macbeth for thinking 'so brainsickly of things'. This regaining of control is also reflected in her imperative language as she orders her stupefied husband around: 'Go, get some water…'; 'Go, carry them and smear the sleepy grooms…'; 'Give me the daggers.'; 'Get on your nightgown.'; 'Be not lost so poorly in your thoughts'. Any decent production will now shift audience focus to Lady Macbeth through a combination of pushing her closer to audience, increasing the intensity of spotlighting on her and most especially through the actor's authoritative body language and witheringly scornful facial expressions. However, her impressive dynamism is not just confined to ordering Macbeth around. When he refuses to return to plant the daggers on Duncan's attendants, she steps in and does it for him but not before chastising him again for being like a child: "tis the eye of childhood / That fears a painted devil'.

This reversal of roles allows Shakespeare to pique audience curiosity again by compelling us to imagine what she's doing off stage. With Lady Macbeth out of the way, Macbeth can now return to centre stage, allowing us access to his mental turmoil. His brief soliloquy is notable for its urgent questions [four in all] and Shakespeare's expert use of halting caesuras, together creating an impression of a man with no answers, struggling to articulate his immense feelings of guilt. Shakespeare also delivers one of his most vibrant visual descriptions of bloodshed [which is saying something given the great torrents of bloody description in the play]: 'my hand will rather / the multitudinous seas incarnadine, / Making the green, one red'. While capturing the irreversible immensity of Macbeth's guilt, Shakespeare also cleverly uses the image of bloody oceans to allow Lady Macbeth to re-enter and for her words to resonate with this image: 'My hands are of your colour, but I shame / To wear a heart so white.'

The relentless knocking [four stage directions within a mere 20 lines] that ends Scene 2 gives it a memorable crescendo of noise. Albeit in a completely different tone, this is continued in the next scene. The sonic assault of Scene 2 is quickly defused at the start of Scene 3 by a drunkern porter, as the play lurches disconcertingly in tone from high tragic intensity to low comedy. Significantly, the source of all the relentless knocking is Macduff, a character whose primary function in the play is to disrupt Macbeth's peace of mind and challenge his successes. While the drunken, hungover porter allows Shakespeare to explicitly reference the dangers of equivocation that echo contextually the Gunpowder Plot of 1605, he also uses him to dissipate the high tension of moral anguish through his bawdy banter with Macduff about drinking, vomiting, pissing and erectile dysfunction. Again, dramatic irony creates a powerful audience effect here as Shakespeare prolongs the discovery of Duncan's [off stage] body for as long as possible to maximise suspense, as well as allowing the audience to scrutinise Macbeth and his reactions. While the previous scenes have only had two speaking characters on stage Scene 3 sees an explosion of characters [presumably entering from all directions] once Macduff raises the alarm. The emotive explosiveness of Macduff's words creates great, if horrifying, excitement, as well as showcasing a deep loyalty towards Duncan that is nakedly contrasted with Macbeth's veiled treachery. The emotive apostrophe and repetition of 'O horror, horror, horror' seems to be a symptom of literally not being able to describe the actual horror of the regicide itself. The hyperbolic metaphor of Duncan as 'The Lord's anointed temple' is taken up [either ironically or guiltily] by Macbeth who describes Duncan's body like that of a saint: 'His silver skin laced with his golden blood.'

Macduff's horrified outrage must be the centrepiece of this scene. He will no doubt visually dominate the stage with plenty of unhinged, frantic stage movements and body language. It would be apt too to push the shifty Macbeths to skulking in the shadows. This would also allow Macduff to be the focus of attention, but also allow them crucial time to formulate appropriate responses. Most productions see them covertly communicating with each other through knowing glances, especially Lady Macbeth who may fear her husband may do something stupid, overwhelmed with guilt as he is. It is telling that both formulate different responses. Macbeth impulsively rushes off stage to murder Duncan's attendants, exemplifying his warrior brutality, whereas she feigns a stereotypically feminine fainting, timing this for when Macduff questions a little too intensely Macbeth's precipitative killing of the attendants. Again, Lady Macbeth proves adept at nimbly adapting to circumstances to further her husband's cause. Additionally, Macduff's cry of 'Wherefore did you so?' is a dangerous public questioning of his host and potential rival. And given that Macbeth has just slain two men, it's just not that clever! Either way, this marks the beginning of Macduff's role in the play as Macbeth's nemesis. Also telling is the way Banquo and Macbeth both vie for control of operations, an insight into their future political rivalry. Both use imperative language becoming of their warrior prestige:

Banquo: Let us meet
            And question this most bloody piece of work
            To know it further.
Macbeth: Let's briefly put on manly readiness
            and meet i'the hall together.

The *Exeunt* would be a suitably dramatic finish to the scene. But Shakespeare further highlights the treacherous political waters in which these noblemen now swim by switching to those most in grief [although you wouldn't think it upon hearing Malcolm's bizarrely pithy 'O, by whom?' when first informed of his father's murder!], and those most in danger: Duncan's sons. Malcolm's departing rhyming couplet connects 'theft' and 'left', pointing to the criminality of Macbeth's murderous actions; the one who has stolen Duncan's life will be left in Scotland, at large. As Prince of Cumberland, Malcolm has a valid grievance as he should ascend to the throne rather than Macbeth. But the couplet rhymes also suggest that by fleeing, it will be all too easy to pin the blame for the murder on Malcolm and Donalbain.

Which is exactly what happens in the rather strange final scene of Act II. Compared to the immediacy, frenetic action and high emotional intensity of the preceding action, Scene 4 unfolds at an almost leisurely pace. Rather than providing action, its function is more to do with exposition, filling the audience

in on how Macbeth has assumed the kingship. Taking place at an unspecified time after the regicide, the immediate dangers have passed and Ross can talk openly with the Old Man about the warping of natural order and harmony since Duncan's murder.

Shakespeare again repeats the pathetic fallacy of the previous scenes to show a Scotland plunged into moral darkness as 'By th'clock 'tis day / And yet dark strangles the travelling lamp'. This use of the violent verb 'strangle' is significant as it connects to Macbeth's unholy violence as well as connecting Duncan to the 'travelling lamp', the visitor who brought prestige and diamonds to Inverness castle only to be brutally snuffed out, a neat antithetical pairing of Dark Macbeth and Light-filled Duncan. Ultimately, just in case we didn't grasp it in the previous scene, the entire situation ''Tis unnatural'. Macbeth's transgression of the natural laws of kinship, loyalty and hosting have caused a dramatic infection of the natural cosmic order. The story of the 'falcon towering in her pride of place' killed by 'a mousing owl' as well as the bizarre cannibalism of 'Duncan's horses' point to personal success for Macbeth, but at a significant cost to wider society.

The openness of the conversation between Ross, the Old Man and eventually Macduff contrasts greatly with the 'curses not loud but deep' and the 'mouth-honour' that characterises Macbeth's tyranny at the end of the play. Again, Macduff, either foolishly or nobly, declares a dangerous intention to avoid Macbeth's coronation. In effect, Macduff challenges the legitimacy of Macbeth's rule and puts himself in great danger. This honesty is punished terribly as we know in Act IV, but ultimately Macduff either cannot or will not play the political game of intrigue. His warning that 'Lest our old robes sit easier than our new' is prophetic in its suggestion that Duncan will turn out to be a better ruler than Macbeth [a provocative and complicated statement that needs careful discussion]. The scene ends with the old Man's promotion of reconciliation rather than rivalry. The warning falls on deaf ears in Macduff's case. Again, individual choices are shown to have terrible collective consequences and another what-if scenario presents itself. What if Macduff and Banquo had been better able to conceal their misgivings with Macbeth, to be uneasy allies rather than honourable rivals? And it is with exactly such misgivings that Banquo begins Act III.

Act Three

The third act of a five-act tragedy is commonly known as the 'climax' or 'turning point'. It is the point of the play where the hero, who has now reached the height of their powers and success, suffers a reversal of fortune, often caused by a tragic flaw in their character, which leads to their tragic downfall and destruction by the end of the play, usually resulting in the tragic hero's death. The third act of Shakespeare's tragedies tend to follow this pattern: we might think of Romeo, recently married to Juliet and at the height of his happiness, killing Paris in the third act of *Romeo and Juliet* and setting off the chain of events that will lead to their double suicide at the end of the play, or Othello, recently married to Desdemona and having enjoyed victory over the Turkish fleet in *Othello*, becoming convinced by Iago's lies about Desdemona's fictitious affair with Cassio in Act III, which leads to him murdering his wife and committing suicide. Arguably, the pattern is slightly different in the plot of *Macbeth*, as it is Macbeth's murder of Duncan in Act II, prompted by ambition and marital insecurity, that leads to his downfall. However, despite this error of judgement, Macbeth's fortunes continue to rise during Act II, a rise which peaks with news of his coronation in Scene 4. It is not until the third act and the establishment of Macbeth as king that we see the reversal of Macbeth's fortunes in the gradual erosion of his authority and power, his mental disintegration and descent into paranoid tyranny. Like the character of Doctor Faustus created by Shakespeare's contemporary, Christopher Marlowe, Macbeth realises in Act III that the thing he sells his soul for does not bring him the happiness and satisfaction he envisaged. By delaying the reversal of fortune until after Macbeth is crowned king, Shakespeare demonstrates how Macbeth's greatest sin was not murder but the usurpation of the kingly role that only God had the right to bestow on man.

Act III Scene 1 starts with a short soliloquy from Banquo. His opening line 'Thou hast it now - King, Cawdor, Glamis, all' demonstrates how Macbeth is now at the zenith of his power and success. However, as in all tragedies, once the hero reaches the top there is only place to go and Shakespeare immediately foreshadows Macbeth's downward trajectory by reminding the audience about the Witches' prophecies to Banquo, that he will be 'the root and father of many kings'. Even at the height of his power, Macbeth's reign is fundamentally destabilised and undermined by the foreknowledge that it is Banquo's progeny that will establish a royal dynasty while Macbeth's line will end with himself. His is essentially a caretaker kingship, operating on borrowed time.

Macbeth himself recognises this threat to his authority in his own soliloquy that mirrors Banquo's, acknowledging how 'To be thus is nothing / but to be safely thus' because his 'fears in Banquo / stick deep'. Macbeth is unable to enjoy any satisfaction from his new kingly position, something he has damned his soul to gain, instead describing it bleakly as 'nothing'. Rather than basking in his status as the most powerful and important man in the whole kingdom, he is racked with anxiety and paranoia regarding Banquo, with the word 'fear' repeated three times within the soliloquy. Macbeth's description of Banquo's 'wisdom', 'valour' and 'royalty of nature' make it sound like Banquo has already supplanted Macbeth as king and the admission of Banquo's superior qualities would no doubt have appealed to James I, who traced his own ancestry back to him.

Banquo's status as 'father to a line of kings' is contrasted with Macbeth's own 'fruitless crown' and 'barren sceptre', which suggests how Banquo not only undermines Macbeth's confidence as king but also the sense of his own masculinity, especially because, as we have previously noted, according to Coppelia Kahn, 'in Shakespeare's world, fatherhood validates a man's identity'. If Macbeth murdered Duncan, in part to prove his manliness to his wife, he finds now that his childless state, contrasted with Banquo's paternality, continues to emasculate him. By the end of the soliloquy, Macbeth's apostrophe 'come fate into the list / And champion me to the utterance' uses personification to challenge fate to a duel and suggests how Macbeth wants to defy the Witches' prophecies and rewrite his destiny, despite everything the Witches predicted having so far come true. It now becomes clear, if it wasn't already, that Macbeth's earlier questioning of Banquo's whereabouts was motivated by Macbeth's machinations to have him murdered and thwart the Witches' prophecies. The scene ends with Macbeth enlisting the two murderers to dispatch Banquo and Fleance and stop the possibility of Banquo's descendants ascending to the throne. Yet even here, Macbeth cannot hide his inner fears, with his portrayal of Banquo as an enemy to the murderers whose 'issue' has held them 'under fortune' and 'beggared yours forever', subconsciously projecting his own insecurities about Banquo and the threat of his offspring to Macbeth's ability to father a royal dynasty. Act III Scene 1 shows us, therefore, how despite now being king and having it all, Macbeth is unable to find any peace in his new position. Instead, he is slowly being isolated and destroyed by the weight of the Witches' prophecies, his paranoia and unravelling mind.

If Scene I demonstrates how kingship is destroying Macbeth's relationship with his best friend, Scene II shifts to showing the effects on his relationship with his wife. No doubt Shakespeare's audience would have criticised Macbeth for the way he allows himself to be manipulated and controlled by his wife, but, undeniably, Shakespeare also communicates a deep sense of love and intimacy between the pair earlier in the play, and there is something compelling and egalitarian in Macbeth's address to his wife in his letter to her as 'my dearest partner of greatness.' However, after the murder of Duncan, this closeness is shattered and the pair drift further apart, becoming isolated from each other.

The scene opens with Lady Macbeth filled with regret for what she and her husband have done, lamenting in a mini-soliloquy how 'Nought's had, all's spent, / Where our desire is got without content. / Tis safer to be that which we destroy / Than by destruction dwell in doubtful joy'. Like Macbeth in the previous scene, she realises that they have gained nothing by killing the king and instead have lost their peace and contentment. She acknowledges it would be even preferable to be, like Duncan, murdered but at peace, than to live in a constant state of anxiety and fear. Yet when Macbeth enters, she immediately assumes her steely, philosophical façade, telling him 'things without all remedy / Should be without regard – what's done is done'. Not only is she unable to be emotionally honest with her husband, her questioning him 'Why do you keep alone?' also suggests how they are struggling to maintain physical proximity with each other. Perhaps the sight of each other proves too much of a painful reminder of their guilt and the love and contentment they have squandered.

In this scene Macbeth is more emotionally honest than his wife his able to be. His admission that it is 'better be with the dead, / Whom we, to gain our peace, have sent to peace / Than on the torture of the mind to lie / In restless ecstasy' echoes and gives voice to Lady Macbeth's inner thoughts that being dead is better than the purgatorial torments of conscience she and her husband now experience but are unable to share. Throughout the play, Shakespeare uses the motif of sleep and sleeplessness to suggest how the Macbeths, through the act of regicide, have not only forfeited inner peace of conscience but also eternal rest and salvation. Lady Macbeth attempts to lift Macbeth's darkened mood, reminding him of the need to 'be bright and jovial among your guests tonight'. He reassures her of his ability to put on a deceptive façade and 'make our faces vizards to our hearts, / Disguising what they are' - his words echoing her earlier advice in Act I to 'look like the innocent flower / but be the serpent under't'. The wording suggests a role reversal; as Macbeth becomes more deceitful and Machiavellian Lady Macbeth loses her hold over him. The growing distance between them is accentuated by the way Macbeth hides his plans to have Banquo murdered from his wife, hinting only at a 'deed of dreadful note', even exhorting her to 'present him eminence' at the banquet despite Macbeth's expectation that Banquo will be killed before then. Macbeth's mental deterioration and the corruption of his psyche can also be detected in the grotesque animal imagery employed in this scene, ranging from 'scorpions' to a 'bat', 'beetle', 'crow' and 'night's black agents', which might also be a reference to the evil spirits

Lady Macbeth evoked earlier in the play. The cumulative effect of the animal imagery gives an incantatory feel to Macbeth's words, echoing the Witches' 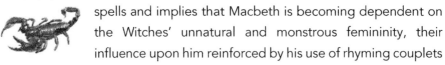 spells and implies that Macbeth is becoming dependent on the Witches' unnatural and monstrous femininity, their influence upon him reinforced by his use of rhyming couplets 'drowse' and 'rouse', 'still' and 'ill' at the end of the scene, paralleling their own style of speech.

Scene 3 continues to trace Macbeth's declining power and authority, albeit his murderous plans are partly successful. The short scene detailing Banquo's murder and Fleance's escape charts Macbeth's first steps into tyrannical leadership, symbolically signalled by the onset of night and darkness. Yet the failure to dispatch Fleance leaves the Witches' prophecy of Banquo's descendants ascending to the throne ominously intact. The presence of a third murderer initially appears mysterious. The point seems to be that Macbeth does not trust the first two murderers sufficiently to get the job done and has therefore sent a third to oversee the assassination. Ironically, it is this decision, born out of paranoia and distrust, that causes the mission's failure, the third murderer's confused question 'Who did strike out the light?' implies that it was a lack of understanding between the three murderers over the details of the plan that has led to Fleance's escape. The more Macbeth tries to take his future into his own hands, conversely, the more he becomes a pawn to destiny and loses control over his own fate and agency.

Scene 4, where Banquo's ghost returns to haunt Macbeth in the midst of his coronation banquet, is the centrepiece of Act III and, to an extent, of the whole play. The ghost, which no one else can see, is often understood as the external manifestation of Macbeth's inner psychological guilt. However, the critic Michael Hawkins has suggested that in feudal societies like Macbeth's Scotland, banquets were symbolic of the host's power to control food supplies and provide provision for his subjects.[21] The significance of Banquo's appearance as a ghost and disruption of the banquet for Hawkins, therefore

---

[21] Hawkins, *History, Politics and Macbeth* in John Russell Brown [ed.] *Focus on Macbeth*.

lies in the way it reveals in a very public setting Macbeth's inadequacy as a king and failure to perform his royal duties. Evidence of Macbeth's decline and reversal of fortune now spreads tangibly from the private sphere into the public world.

The scene starts badly for Macbeth. His act to 'play the humble host' quickly collapses when the murderers arrive and tell him Fleance has escaped. The fragility of Macbeth's mental and emotional state is exposed by his reaction, 'Then comes my fit again'. Shakespeare's use of alliteration in Macbeth's complaint that 'now I am cabined, cribbed, confined, bound in / to saucy

 doubts and fears' emphasises Macbeth's claustrophobic sense of being trapped by his fears as well as the wider workings of fate that he seems powerless to escape. Things get even worse for Macbeth with the arrival of Banquo's ghost. The action of the ghost entering and sitting at Macbeth's place at the table symbolises the way Banquo's children will supplant Macbeth's royal position. Macbeth's reaction to the ghost reveals his paranoia, 'Which of you have done this?' and his futile attempts to suppress his guilt 'Thou canst not say I did it'. As after the murder of Duncan, Lady Macbeth attempts to take control of the situation, her words 'My lord is often thus, and hath been from his youth,' attempts to persuade the guests Macbeth's behaviour is a symptom of a lifelong condition. She also reverts to the strategy of emasculating Macbeth that had been so effective in convincing him to go through with Duncan's murder, asking him whether he is 'quite unmanned in folly?' Even in death, Banquo's paternal status and role as 'father to a line of kings' continues to undermine Macbeth's authority and subvert his masculinity. Macbeth responds to his wife that he would be man enough to fight a living enemy, even 'the Russian bear, the armed rhinocerosos, th'Hyrcan tiger' but it is Banquo's unnaturalness, the 'horrible shadow' and 'unreal mockery' that has unmanned him.

The disruption to the natural order, indicated by Macbeth's lines 'The time has been / That when the brains were out, the man would die…But now they

rise again' also suggests how the social and natural worlds are intimately connected through God's hierarchy of the Divine Right of Kings and the Great Chain of Being. The disturbance in one realm, brought about by the murder of God's divinely appointed king, has led to rupture and chaos in the other. The lexis of disorder that runs through Macbeth's language in this scene, evident in words such as 'infirmity', 'tremble', 'unreal', 'displaced', 'broke', disorder', 'at odds', 'lack' and 'self-abuse' also highlights how keenly the disruption is felt by Macbeth on an individual level. Despite the awful consequences of his actions, by the end of the scene he acknowledges it is too late to repair or reverse his moral decline. His admission to his wife that 'I am in blood / Stepped in so far that should I wade no more, / Returning were as tedious as go o'er' increases the sense of tragic inevitability as he advances towards his destruction. The decision to return 'to the weird sisters' further emphasises waning powers and loss of control as he abdicates the masculine authority of kingship for the unnatural and supernatural femininity represented by the Witches.

In the final scene, Shakespeare widens the perspective, showing us Macbeth's declining fortunes as viewed by his subjects. Scene VI opens with Lennox discussing Macbeth's reign with another lord. Lennox's sarcastic tone as he ridicules how Duncan's death 'did grieve Macbeth' and how his killing of Duncan's servants was 'nobly done' suggests suspicion of Macbeth's guilt has now become widespread, leading him to become a figure of mockery and resentment among his subjects. However, Lennox uses multiple rhetorical questions to hint at meanings that are opposite to what he is literally saying, implying the tyrannical hold that Macbeth continues to exert over his people. The Lord's response to Lennox that Macduff has fled to England to join forces with Malcolm, who is raising an army to attack Macbeth, gives a wider sense of the forces beginning to amass against him, further undermining his power and authority. The reference to Edward, the King of England, as 'the holy king' also reminds the audience that Macbeth's unholy kingship lacks legitimacy and approval from God. From the high point of Macbeth's coronation, Act III shows the audience Macbeth's gradual reversal of fortune and declining powers. There will still be some distance to travel until the tragic denouement in Act V, but the inexorable downhill journey has now been set in motion.

Act Four

Although it contains some action, notably the murder of the Macduffs, the function of Act IV is really to build up to the play's climax. Shakespeare is tightly packing the powder-keg so that there can be a tremendous explosion

in Act V: The Witches' scene fortifies Macbeth's hubris and ensures that he will not yield to Malcolm's forces; the murder of the Macduffs both dramatises Macbeth's descent into tyranny and sharpens Macduff's appetite for revenge. The Act ends with the forces or order amassing, with a promise to overthrow Macbeth, anticipating the violent action of Act V.

From a structural perspective, *Macbeth* follows a strikingly similar pattern to *Richard III*, an earlier 'history' play in which Shakespeare constructs the Tudor Myth surrounding the villainous nature of a past king in order to flatter the current monarch. In both plays, the first half is dedicated to the increasing power and ambition of the tragic hero [or anti-hero]; they obtain the crown at the climactic mid-point; the moment they become king is then the precise moment of the downfall of their fortunes. Both kings suffer from the same plague of psychological torment which ultimately makes them the architects of their own demise.

Act IV in both plays marks the descent of both kings into evil with the murder of innocents as a result of their desperation to keep hold of the power they have gained and desire to eliminate all opposition, whatever the cost. Famously in *Richard III* our anti-hero sends murderers to kill the two young princes [his nephews] in the tower; a moment in history which has sparked much intrigue and controversy, but which suited Shakespeare's purposes in constructing a barbarous villain who must be slain by the virtuous Henry Tudor. Macbeth's parallel scene is, of course, the murder of all Macduff's 'pretty ones', as the latter so tenderly and heartbreakingly describes them, 'all my pretty chickens and their dam at one fell swoop'. Fuelled by the Witches' prophecy to 'beware Macduff, Thane of Fife' at the start of Act IV, Macbeth sends murderers to butcher the entire family.

Macbeth's treachery is emphasised by the discussion between Lady Macduff and her son before the murderers' imminent arrival. Macduff's son is shown to be wise beyond his years as he discusses the nature of treachery with his mother. He asks who 'must hang' the trailers who swear and lie, in reference to his father who has fled Scotland as a 'traitor'. When she answers, 'Why, the honest men', he reasons 'the liars and swearers are / fools, for there are liars and / swearers enough to beat the / honest men and hang up them'. The bleak assessment of the humanity he has encountered thus far in his short life demonstrates the sickness which has pervaded Scotland as a result of Macbeth's brutal  reign. Even a child can testify that the lines between good and evil have become so blurred that truly 'honest' men are few and far between.

This debate also sums up the interesting position that Macduff holds within the play; as the ultimate king slayer of Macbeth, he also commits regicide. This places him in a morally uncertain, grey area, as whilst Macbeth's reign has not been ordained by God due to his own regicide, he has still been crowned. It is important that Macduff is driven by a personal desire for revenge rather than political gain when he kills Macbeth and Shakespeare sets up the massacre of his family to firmly establish the need for vengeance. It also closes a fateful loop that the Witches set up at the start of Act IV when they warn Macbeth to 'beware Macduff'; arguably if they had not sown this seed of paranoia, Macbeth would not have been driven to order the deaths of his offspring. Without this motivation, whilst Macduff's loyalty still lay with Malcolm, would he have fought so ferociously and successfully? Thus is the circular nature of the events which the Witches set in motion; the ultimate self-fulfilling prophecy.

Whilst it has been useful to draw comparisons between Richard III and Macbeth in terms of their similar character arcs as villains, it is yet more useful to appreciate the key differences between the characters as constructed by Shakespeare to suit his differing purposes. Richard III from the outset is introduced to the audience as the devil incarnate; his opening soliloquy draws the audience into his brazenly murderous plans. To flatter Elizabeth I and reinforce the Tudor position on the throne for Shakespeare it is vital that the audience knows Henry Tudor is justified in killing Richard. By the time Shakespeare wrote *Macbeth*, a new monarch was in place, with diverging interests and motivations. James I had recently survived an assassination attempt with the gunpowder plot, so the play had to reinforce the sanctity of the Divine Right of Kings and assert the social order. As has been discussed elsewhere in this guide, Macbeth is punished for committing regicide and the message surrounding the gunpowder plot is clear and even alluded to directly through Lady Macbeth's reference to becoming the 'innocent flower' with the 'serpent under it'.

The reinforcement of the social order is also established through the representation of the Witches. Given James I's portrayal of the supernatural in his tract *Daemonolgie*, Shakespeare must weave the influence of the occult into Macbeth's motivation and influence. Rather than introducing us to a firmly established villain, Shakespeare presents Macbeth initially as a hero. Whilst his capacity and potential for corruption are open to debate, he is generally accepted as a good man whose meeting with the Witches is fatal. Finally, it could be argued that *Macbeth* operates to reinforce traditional gender roles by portraying both the Witches and Lady Macbeth as such dangerous and corrupting forces. In a society which has seen the long, glorious and successful reign of a female monarch, it would not be a great stretch of the imagination to consider that men and women could see the skills and talents female leadership had to offer. Many students argue in essays about Lady Macbeth that her behaviour is 'shocking' and 'unexpected' to a Jacobean audience. An alternative argument could be that women during the Elizabethan era became more powerful and vocal, and that James I's obsession with finding and condemning witches was an attempt to suppress these female voices.

Whilst a detailed examination of Act IV Scene I takes place in our essay on the Witches, it is useful here to examine its purpose following the crowning of Macbeth. The first meeting of the Witches establishes the prophecy that he will become king. As he has now become king, Macbeth immediately lacks direction and purpose. His desire to visit the Witches again is symptomatic of his decline in power and his lack of agency, despite having the most powerful position in Scotland. Each  subsequent scene in this act reinforces Macbeth's decline. Scene II is the enactment of his grossly paranoid over-reaction to the Witches' instruction to 'beware Macduff'. Scene III cross-cuts to England and sets up the pivotal relationship between Malcolm and Macduff: the kingslayer and the subsequent king who promises to restore the natural order. Once again Macbeth does not appear and he is notable for his absence. He is only on stage in this act in the first scene during which he receives the apparitions by the Witches and acts upon them blindly and without reason. From a practical point of view, this gap allows the actor playing Macbeth to recover and get ready for his dramatic finale. Symbolically it suggests a shifting of power away from the Macbeths and onto the forces that will unseat them.

Act IV ends with a scene which is sometimes passed over due to its lack of drama and excitement. Whilst lengthy scenes of political discussion are not unusual in Shakespeare's plays, it does stand out as unusual in *Macbeth*. Up until this point the action has moved swiftly and the audience has been treated to the equivalent of a modern-day nail-biting thriller with intrigue, suspense and drama. However, this scene has multiple functions: It almost entirely consists of a conversation between Malcolm and Macduff in which Macduff's loyalty is sorely tested. Interestingly, though, it is not Maduff's loyalty to Malcolm which is being tested, it's his loyalty to Scotland. There is a heavy sense of dramatic irony pervading the conversation, as the audience have just witnessed the horrifying murder of Macduff's son and the murderers persuing his wife with instructions to kill the entire household. We know that Macduff will soon hear this news, so Shakespeare is playing rather a cruel trick as Malcolm expounds at length over his worthiness as king. A strong sense of irony pervades much of what he says; 'You have loved [Macbeth] well. / He hath not touched you yet'. We are reminded that until this point Macduff had been a loyal servant of Macbeth, just as Banquo had been, and that Macbeth's murder of Duncan cost him many good friends. As an audience we also know that Macbeth has indeed 'touched' Macduff in the most painful of ways, and the audience will be poised and waiting for the inevitable messenger to deliver this fateful news.

Macduff's integrity comes under scrutiny during the previous act and very early in this scene Malcolm questions whether Macduff might double-cross him and offer him up to Macbeth as a 'weak, poor innocent lamb / To appease an angry god'. The juxtaposition created here is interesting as Malcolm is exaggerating his weakness and purity in contrast to Macbeth's hubristic and blasphemous portrayal as a deity. By killing Duncan, which both men believe he has, and installing himself as king, Macbeth has indeed taken on the role of God. Macduff's simple and categorical response is convincing; 'I am not treacherous'. The ensuing conversation proves that this indeed is the case. Malcolm tests Macduff by arguing that even if he does succeed in overthrowing Macbeth, Scotland shall 'have more vices than it had before' with himself as king. To the audience, this declaration would be quite a revelation, as the predictable narrative arc places Malcolm firmly back on the throne with the inevitable restoration of the equilibrium. A detailed analysis of this exchange can be found in the Macduff character essay, but suffice to say that Scotland will not, in fact, be plagued with vices with Malcolm as king. He was setting out to determine how far Macduff would be prepared to compromise on his morality as king in order to install him on the throne in place of Macbeth. Ultimately, Macduff cannot accept the level of depravity which Malcolm ascribes to himself and declares him 'unfit to live', let alone govern. This is exactly the response Duncan is after; he wants Macduff to desire what is best for Scotland, as opposed to installing an unworthy ruler for his own political advancement.

This brings us to the central function of this scene; establishing Duncan's worthiness as king and hammering home the qualities of kingship which are most desireable. James I's essay 'The True Law', with which Shakespeare would certainly have been familiar, sets out the ultimate Divine Right of Kings, but also the responsibilities that this places on the monarch and the subsequent qualities which a king must hold. Using Duncan as a mouthpiece within this exchange, Shakespeare lists those qualities almost as an echo of King James I's ideas: 'justice, verity, temperance, stableness, / Bounty, perseverance, mercy, lowliness, / Devotion, patience, courage, fortitude'. Despite his evident weaknesses, it is clear that Duncan had these kingly qualities and later in the exchange Malcolm confesses his subterfuge and claims to also possess them. We are now firmly set up to restore the natural order after all. The end of the scene brings the moment the audience have been anticipating as Ross arrives to deliver the news of Macduff's family's slaughter. Whilst initially Ross states they are 'well' and 'at peace', this is an evasion which only delays the inevitable news and further draws out the tension and suspense. Ross's words are chilling 'your wife and babes / Savagely slaughter'd: to relate the manner, / Were, on the quarry of these murder'd deer / To add the death of you'. As the majority of the murders took place off stage, the audience are left to imagine the horrors that were inflicted upon them. Whilst Macbeth has been our tragic hero through the first half of the play, we are more than ready to witness his demise at the hands of a vengeful Macduff. As he points out, the fact that Macbeth has no children means that Macduff will never truly exact revenge; he will have to satisfy himself with restoring the natural order to Scotland by displacing the tyrant and using his grief as the 'whetstone to [his] sword'.

Act Five

Act V is quite a different audience experience than the preceding Act. Act IV has only three scenes, two substantially lengthy ones hinged around an episode of pure amorality. The structural logic of Act IV [unstable tyrant mocked by supernatural evil; his shame is transformed into amoral murder and the flourishing of moral resistance] drives rapid-fire scene changes with seemingly unstoppable momentum of Act V. If Act IV is the powder keg being lit, Act V is the explosion of chaos. Chaos that must be endured before order can be restored. Act V has nine scenes in total, most no longer than 30 lines, and they swiftly alternate between the two conflicting sides: Macbeth at Inverness Castle and Malcolm's invading forces, the rescuers of Scotland.

Shakespeare's dramatic strategy renders Macbeth strangely passive and Malcolm antithetically active as he surges towards Dunsinane. Malcolm's forward momentum is matched by Macbeth's shrinking power and confidence. As political rivals the pendulum firmly swings Malcolm's way, a development reinforced by his authoritative but steady command of the liberators. Macbeth, in contrast, oscillates between downtrodden nihilism and clamorous bravado.

Ultimately, the rapid progression of Act V, with the noose tightening around Macbeth's defiant neck, is most satisfying for an audience straining to see moral order restored and goodness [a dangerous term to use in this play for sure!] rewarded. The double avengers, Macduff and Malcolm, have right on their side and their victory is both political and moral. The swiftness of Act V also betrays a type of desire to get out of this amoral universe as quickly as possible, as if the audience itself can be infected by the onstage events in the same way Macbeth's actions infect [or is it the Witches' malevolence?] the natural order of things. Act V also reveals Macbeth's acute nihilism. Despite the comforts of the Witches' protecting prophecies, there is a distinct feeling that he wants it all to end. Power has not turned out the way he envisioned it at all and his plunging into evil, rather than making him appreciate more the trappings of personal success, has reduced all life to a jaded numbness. It also feels like he too wants to exit the play world, along with the audience, as swiftly as he can.

Typically, in a play of continuous unpredictable shifts, where we would expect Act V to begin with Malcolm and Macduff or even Macbeth, Shakespeare catches the audience off-guard. The play switches from bright English sunshine to Scottish night, from exterior to interior, from hopeful liberation to hopeless entrapment, from male togetherness to female isolation. Lady Macbeth has essentially disappeared since the banquet scene in Act III as her once weaker husband surpasses and dwarfs her in his wholehearted embrace of evil. Her return in Act V is quite a surprise and this surprise is intensified by her shocking mental deterioration. The once steely, cold-hearted opportunist is almost unrecognisable. Now she is a pitiful, haunted and broken woman. This fall from power is also reflected linguistically in Shakespeare's use of unpredictable prose rather than the more controlled rhythm of blank verse. It may also come as a shock that it is this first scene that is the most emotionally engaging, and probably even the most humane episode in the concluding act, which makes the rest of the act tonally contrasting for the audience. Lady Macbeth's scene's slow-paced, static agony is distinctly at odds with the rapid, dynamic pace of action that follows.

Lady Macbeth's mental distresses and tortured guilt are highly ironic given her critical reproaching of her husband in Act II. However, while his guilt in Act II was construed as masculine weakness, her feminine guilt is much more devastating is its discordant power. While his was temporary, hers is devastatingly permanent. Lady Macbeth's revelation of her inner turmoil delivers the type of pathos one normally associates with the tragic hero, a pathos that is denied to Macbeth later in the act. Again Shakespeare destabilises our expectations, even at genre level. In this scene, her lamentations are transmitted via sleepwalking, where the deceitful veils of conscious performance cannot hide the truth. This is significant in a world where deceit permeates everything, from the Witches to Macbeth to Lennox, and worryingly, even to Malcolm. This unease with naked revelation of truth is articulated structurally in this scene as Lady Macbeth's confession, if it can be recognised as such, is bookended by the cautious interactions of her attendant and the doctor. The doctor's dramatic function here is to comment on the shocking narrative that Lady Macbeth's fragmented ramblings form, confirmation of a narrative surely rumoured throughout Scotland. He describes her sleepwalking as 'a great perturbation in nature' and her mind as 'infected'. What is also striking, and this must be a sign of the paranoia that reigns under Macbeth's tyranny, is how both observers are scared to admit what they have seen, as if being a witness is synonymous with being an accomplice. The Gentlewoman 'will not report after her [...] neither to you, nor anyone, having no witness to confirm my speech'. Similarly, the Doctor can 'think but dare not speak'. In a tyranny, then, deceit is not so much of a moral failing as a practical tool of survival.

Lady Macbeth enters 'with a taper,' a prop that is both practical and symbolic. A great reversal has occurred as her invocation of the dark spirits of Act I has been replaced with its opposite; she clings to a slender candle, as its light as vulnerable and unstable as she has become. It also resonates with her husband's memorable later soliloquy about the ultimate futility and meaningless of life later in the act: 'Out, out, brief candle'. This is the only remaining connection between them. Whereas the play had earlier presented a dynamic couple, partners 'in greatness,' by Act V their relationship is another form of deception. As Macbeth has spectacularly waxed, she has spectacularly waned and the human cost to their relationship is total. She 'by self and violent hands / Took off her life' alone, wracked by guilt, while her husband is so consumed with the consolidation of power that in Scene 5 he can barely be bothered to respond emotionally to her tragic demise: 'She should have died hereafter'. Such numbed nihilism that might explain why audience sympathy can be felt for her, but not, in the end, for him. A key question, of course, is whether this pathetic episode is enough to redeem her, given her previous ruthlessness. Answers on a very large postcard to that one, please! The test of any actor playing Lady Macbeth is whether they can secure audience sympathy in a mere 45 lines. One can guarantee that the use of makeup will ensure a haunted expression, the lighting will be dramatic, the nightdress costume possibly symbolic [White? Black? Red polka dots?], the physical gesturing suitably distressed. Possibilities abound.

However, despite such stagecraft opportunities, it is Shakespeare's language that must bear the heaviest load. And related to this must be the delivery of the lines themselves. This is an episode that requires very careful emotional calibration. The repetitive and not overly informative 'Oh, oh, oh' and "To bed, to bed, to bed' are key moments which must respectively capture great existential anguish and complete brokenness. Around these emotional peaks lie a collection of sentence fragments that are just cohesive enough to convey the disorder of her mind. The apparent replaying of the regicide and Banquo's murder is characterised by insistent repetition - 'Come, come, come, come, give me your hand', stuttering caesuras - 'Out, damned spot: out, I say. One; two. Why then 'tis the time to do't. Hell is murky' and a clamorous questioning that echoes Macbeth's stunned self-questioning after his killing of Duncan in Act II: 'A soldier and afeard?'; 'What need we fear?'; 'Who would have thought the old man to have so much blood in him?'; 'Where is she now?'; 'Will these hands ne'er be clean?'. Clearly, she has no answers to her questions and her spiritual torment must continue until she can bear it no more. Another linguistic aspect of her speech is the distinctly child-like way in which Lady Macbeth speaks. Her sentences structures are simple and short, such as 'Hell is murky' and Shakespeare even provides the sound of a child's nursery rhyme: 'The Thane of Fife had a wife' – all of which bestow on her a pitiful vulnerability, if not a broken innocence. There is also the direct simplicity of her imaginative descriptions: the visuals of the 'damned spot' and the olfactory power of 'Here's the smell of the blood still'. Shakespeare's use of the adjective 'little' to describe her hand further amplifies her pathetic destruction. Her insistent imperative of 'To bed, to bed' as she exits is both practical [as in she needs to stop sleepwalking] and symbolic [the big sleep of death awaits her as suicide looms as the only solution to her suffering]. After this scene will come an explosion of conflict in the public world of men, which only increases the terrible intimacy of our watching Lady Macbeth's private self-destruction.

The rest of Act V concerns itself with the battle between good and evil. What changes in Act V is that both these forces are given equal weighting, rather than the extended access to Macbeth's immoral mentality, which has dominated the play thus far. Act V also sees the play come full circle as the widescale breakdown of social order seen in Act I returns. The chaos of uprising and revolt was particularly one-sided at the start of the play, whereas

 here it is much more even-handed. From one perspective this is positive; good has regained balance with bad. But from a more pessimistic perspective it renders them unsettlingly similar. This is not quite as far-fetched as it sounds

as we shall see in the problematic ending to the play. However, before this, Act V efficiently brings the two foes together as embodied in the single, hand-to-hand combat between Macbeth and Macduff. Shakespeare also subtly differentiates between the two sides. The liberators are characterised by a straightforward determination to right wrongs. Malcolm, in league with Old Siward, is presented as an effective and level-headed leader. He is an able military strategist whose imperative language conveys authority: 'Let every soldier hew him down a bough / And bear't before him'. He also is clear-sighted in the conflict that awaits, coolly assessing Macbeth's situation: 'none serve him but constrained things / whose hearts are absent too'. Despite the claim that 'revenges burn in them, for their dear causes' it is Macduff who burns with righteous fury, rather than Malcolm and surely he has as much personal vengeance to exact as Macduff. It must be remembered, however, Malcolm's emotionally underwhelming response to his father's murder and more recently his cunning testing of Macduff's commitment to Scotland. Every time Malcolm's forces arrive on stage they bring with them an undeniable sonic energy of *'alarums,'* and *'drums and colours'* that suggests they possess the vital impulse needed for victory.

In great contrast, Macbeth, is presented as a man unhinged. Erratically he swings from exhausted hopelessness to vociferous bravado. His treatment of his subordinates is particularly poor and a useful way of encouraging the audience to turn against him. His taunting of the clearly terrified young servant is cruel and spiteful: 'Go prick thy face, and over-red thy fear, / Thou lily-livered boy'. His treatment of the doctor treating his wife is also disrespectful and taunting: 'Throw physic to the dogs, I'll none of it'. There is great irony in his demand that the doctor 'cast / the water of my land, find her disease / and purge it to a sound and pristine health' as it is so obvious to the audience that Macbeth himself is the disease. Furthermore, Shakespeare allows the audience to change sides [like Macbeth's demoralised men, Lennox and 'the thanes [who] fly from' him] by also putting the same language of illness and restorative medicine in the mouths of the liberators. Caithness in Scene 2 describes Malcolm's invading forces as 'the medicine of the sickly weal / And with him pour in our country's purge / Each drop of us'.

Malcolm's forces are characterised by the 'many unrough youths, that even now / Protest their first of manhood'. It is a distinctly young army, implying Malcolm embodies a new generation of Scots that will herald a new age. It seems that the feeble old age of Duncan, and now the egotistical middle age of Macbeth must give way to allow youthful, but tentative idealism to flourish. The language of natural growth is also notable in this scene as Lennox describes the patriotic bloodshed required to 'dew the sovereign flower, and drown the weeds'. Such noble courage is exemplified by Young Siward's brave death at Macbeth's hand in Scene 6, a death accepted by his father with stoic calm: 'They say he parted well and paid his score, / And so God be with him'.

Self-sacrifice for king and country is the complete opposite to Macbeth's sacrificing of others for his own personal gain. The unpalatable reality of his 'distempered cause' and his unfitness to rule, now castigated as more than a 'dwarfish thief', ensures this becomes a conflict where victory for Malcolm is the only morally acceptable outcome. Despite his petty unkindness and his instability, evinced in particular by his repeated orders to Seyton to put on his armour only to then immediately demand it be taken off in Scene 3, Macbeth articulates an exhausted regret at the way things have turned out. His devastating soliloquies in Scenes 3 and 5 are a much truer reflection of his psyche than his bold, martial proclamations to 'send out more horses, skirr the country round' and to 'hang out our banners on the outward wall'. Amidst the chaos of military preparation Shakespeare never loses sight of the emotional distress his anti-hero suffers. In Scene 3 he realises that the 'honour, love, obedience, troops of friends' owed to a loyal, long-serving servant to Scotland can never materialise. Instead he must make do with 'curses not loud but deep, mouth honour, breath / Which the heart would fain deny, and dare not'. Scene 5 delivers the famous 'Tomorrow' soliloquy, in which life is unforgettably dismissed as 'a tale / Told by an idiot, full of sound and fury / Signifying nothing'. Interestingly, Shakespeare allows Macbeth to voice this existential despair before a messenger comes to obliterate one of the protecting prophecies he hides behind: Birnam Wood is indeed advancing on Dunsinane. While a shocking revelation that shows how much of a plaything he was for the Witches or the 'fiend / That lies like truth' it does at least spur Macbeth on to a final act of energetic violent, and arguably even heroic defiance: 'come wrack / At least we'll die with harness on our back.'

Which brings Act V nicely to the long-awaited confrontation between Macduff, burning with revenge, and Macbeth a man with little left to live for. Macduff has not been reputed in the play as a warrior to match Macbeth but perhaps animated by moral outrage, this classic avenger figure more than holds his own in their duel. It is a moment of dramatic climax which Shakespeare makes more powerful than merely the long-awaited battle between evil 'hell-hound' and wronged avenger, for here he delivers the stunning revelation that 'Macduff was from his mother's womb / Untimely ripped'. For first-time spectators this is surely a jaw-dropping moment, one that strips away the last vestiges of Macbeth's supernatural protection, allowing Macduff to brand him a coward. Macbeth is stunned and his unwillingness to fight is not cowardice rather the shocked reaction of a man realising how much he has been bewitched and manipulated by 'juggling fiends [...] that palter with us in a double sense'. Shakespeare cleverly increases the tension by making the audience wait to see how the conflict is resolved; he ignites a second round of duelling that takes itself off stage then back on stage before Macbeth's dramatic death.

Narrative resolution and moral satisfaction are delivered with the killing of Macbeth. So why do we need another scene? While Scene 9 confirms what we already know, i.e. that Malcom has won [Old Siward tells us this in Scene 7: 'the castle's gently rendered'] it does not add any further comfort to the audience. Visually it is exciting; a crowded stage that seems like a national address and then the dramatically gory entrance of Macduff with Macbeth's head. However, while Malcolm's acceptance speech promising the 'calling home our exiled friends abroad' and the re-branding of thanes as earls ['the  first that ever Scotland / In such an honour named'] feels reassuring, there is something underwhelming about it all. One source of this underwhelming is that we have spent so little time with Malcolm and have not been as closely invested in them as with Macbeth. In fact, we know more about his saintly father Duncan than we do about Malcolm. Another source of unease is the credibility of Malcolm, an inexperienced, unworldly virgin, as king. His 16 line exit speech is hardly inspirational stuff. Rather like his command of the liberating forces, it is efficient in its brevity, cool-headed and functional, but devoid of the searing imagery of Macbeth's most memorable utterances. The lack of rhyming [only the final four lines rhyme] relegates it to frankly, pretty bland, uninspiring stuff. Retrospectively Macbeth's tortured evil seems more dynamic and alluring. Certainly he was more exciting to follow! And he didn't abscond when the going got tough: once Duncan is murdered, rather unheroically Malcolm fled with Donalbain because of the 'daggers in men's smiles'. Additionally, compared with the warrior prestige of Macbeth, Banquo, Old Siward and to some extent Macduff, Malcolm displays no martial excellence. Dunsinane is taken and he is invited inside by Old Siward, the battle is won almost for him and Macduff proclaims him new king of Scotland. Of course, this may well be Shakespeare's point: political strategy married to the threat, or at worst, sparing use of violent force is always more preferable to unrestrained brutality.

There are further problems. In a gruesome echo of the quashing of Macdonald's uprising in Act I, Macduff has become Macbeth, brandishing his defeated rival's severed head. The symbolic decapitation of 'this dead butcher' renders Macduff as just another violent dog-of-war serving a more powerful man. But who's to say that Macduff does not possess dangerous ambition either? Maybe loss of a family will now see a devotion to political life? It must also be pointed out that the Witches win. They are never punished or held to account – they remain powerful, ungoverned and at large. Malcolm's outwitting of Macduff in King Edward's English court also shows the triumph of deception and, perhaps, political manipulation will form a cornerstone of Malcolm's reign. Certainly, a pessimistic reading of the ending will hear Malcolm's words as ringing hollow: he promises a new beginning but only through the use of familiar old weapons - deceit and violence. To aggravate this, the widespread social upheaval, the beheading of opponents rewarded with political favour and the celebratory 'hail!' proclamations [that unsettlingly echoes the Witches] all suggest a returning cycle of events. Is this truly a new beginning or just the beginning of a new depressingly familiar cycle? Maybe this is unfair: Malcolm's deception serves the state whereas Macbeth's deception only served himself. Maybe Shakespeare's message is one of political pragmatism: deceit is a useful weapon, as long as egotistical ambition remains subservient to collective stability.

The soliloquies

Who are we? What we say and do or what we think and feel? Is the core of identity external and revealed by our social interactions or internal and revealed by what's really going on inside our heads?

What's the function of a soliloquy? This dramatic device is the equivalent of extended interior monologue in novels; it takes us right into the mind of a character. Shakespeare is particularly adept at showing us how characters change and adapt themselves in different contexts. Often the public self is itself a kind of performance, a playing of a role. Think, for instance, of how Macbeth takes on the role of king or how he continues to play being Banquo's friend while secretly planning to murder him, or how Lady Macbeth plays the role of welcoming hostess to Duncan. This public self is often a mask or façade and contrasts starkly with a hidden self that is only revealed during private interaction with a trusted partner, friend, lover or spouse. For Macbeth this confidante is, of course, his wife. Together they conspire in secret while presenting an innocent appearance to the outside world. This private/ public duality of characters is another form of the doubling that so pervades this play.

However, even with his wife, Macbeth finds himself taking on or being manipulated into taking on particular roles. When she persuades him against his better judgement to carry out the regicide, for instance, she forces him back into the role of fearless male warrior. Moreover, as the play progresses, as we note elsewhere in this guide, Macbeth consults his wife less and even excludes her from some of his most significant decisions. Though after the murder of Duncan both Macbeths become locked into a living nightmare, for both of them the experience is shared, but also horribly individual. So, arguably in the soliloquies we see the purest expression of a character's true self, character unburdened by the obligations of social interaction.

The soliloquies in *Macbeth* are not as numerous or extensive as those in *Hamlet*, the play that features Shakespeare's most famous soliloquy. The contrast highlights Shakespeare's greater interest in Hamlet's mind and the Danish prince's character as a thinker. Macbeth is less philosophical, less interested in challenging the fundamental ideas that underpin experience. On the whole, his soliloquies reveal his turbulent and increasingly anguished state of mind. Shakespeare gives Macbeth only has four shortish soliloquies and his wife two. Importantly, one of Macbeth's main foils, Banquo, is also afforded a short soliloquy at the start of Act III.

For reasons we will outline later in our essay on his character, Banquo could, potentially, be seen as an opposite of Macbeth and as the true hero of the play. Crucially, he does nothing to bring the Witches' prophecies to fruition, despite the apparent benefits to himself and he remains loyal to Duncan, claiming after the King's murder that he will 'against the undivulged pretence' of 'treacherous malice' fight. [As we will learn later, Shakespeare has good reason to present Banquo in such a favourable light.]

Banquo's soliloquy has two, contradictory effects: On the one hand, it brings the audience closer to him as a character, granting us privileged access to the inner workings of his mind. But on the other hand, this access reveals Banquo's moral equivocation. Though he is deeply suspicious that Macbeth has 'playdst most foully' for the crown, he is not going to reveal this, yet, nor do anything about it, in spite of the noble sentiments he has expressed in public. Why? Because he has a vested interest and hopes to benefit from Macbeth's crime. Banquo's hesitation to act and his equivocation seal his doom and make him culpable for allowing Macbeth to get away with his subsequent tyranny. Hence Shakespeare makes sure that, though he has noble qualities, Banquo doesn't eclipse Macbeth as a character.

Lady Macbeth's first soliloquy, in Act I Scene 5, establishes some crucial ideas about both her and her husband. Specifically, she fears his 'nature' is 'too full o' th' milk of human kindness' to carry out the regicide and that Macbeth is too upright and honourable to 'play false', observations that reflect back to reveal her own more ruthless and duplicitous character. Lady Macbeth's soliloquy is more like a speech to herself, a kind of pep talk, rather than an expression of spontaneous thought. Although she is excited by her husband's news, Shakespeare has her thinking coolly in coherent, controlled and business-like terms, with a clear sequence of ideas. She shows herself to be perceptive, ambitious and resolute. Her style is distinctly declarative, in contrast, for instance, to a character such as Hamlet whose soliloquies are riddled with questions.

In her infamous second soliloquy the extent of her determination to help her husband to the crown becomes clear. Chillingly, she calls on evil spirits to rid herself of her humanity and specifically of her womanly virtues, such as compassion, kindness and pity, and, in effect, she invites them to transform her into a fourth witch. Notably, although she says she will act to help her husband she imagines herself at the centre of the action: Duncan's entrance will be under her battlements and it will be her 'knife' that makes the fatal wound.

Although in both soliloquies Lady Macbeth sounds formidably resolute, there is a sense in which she is trying to crush her own doubts and silence her own unquiet conscience. In the first she avoids direct reference to murder and, in the second, she needs the spirits to prevent 'compunctious visitings of nature' getting in the way of her plans. Moreover, she doesn't really want to see the harm she intends to do, evoking 'thick night' so that 'my keen knife see not the wound'. And notice too that she imagines heaven [or her own suppressed conscience] might 'cry' out 'Hold! Hold!'.

Different actors will play Lady Macbeth's soliloquies in different ways. She could be played as grimly and fanatically determined, but the speeches are more powerful if there's a hint of self-doubt and, in the second one, if her excitement is mixed with genuine terror at what she's doing, i.e. conjuring wicked spirits. A quick google search will allow you to compare different versions, but for our money, it's hard to beat Judi Dench's performance.

We've traced some similar expressions of self-conflicts and attempts to suppress them within Macbeth himself in sections of this book examining stage directions [see p.20] and Shakespeare's use of language [p.60]. The same self-quarrelling patterns are also apparent in Macbeth's first extended interior monologue in Act I Scene 7. Most notably, as we've already mentioned, like his wife, he repeatedly, almost obsessively, avoids naming the sin he is about to commit, trying to bury it under the innocuous pronoun 'it'. In the rest of his first soliloquy, with a cool rationality that subsequent events will topple Macbeth argues against himself, outlining many strong reasons why he should not carry out the heinous murder: He should wait, rather than 'jump the life to come'; by killing Duncan he would set a precedent for his own murder; he owes Duncan a 'double' allegiance as 'kinsman', 'subject' and 'host'. Moreover, Duncan's 'virtues / Will plead like angels, trumpet-tongued, against / The deep damnation' of his murder, euphemistically called his 'taking-off'.

Obviously, the heavenly imagery in these lines counterbalances the hellish imagery that dominates most of the play. Events will prove Macbeth right; the murder will indeed awaken pity and, though it is delayed until Act V, animate

 a virtuous revenging force, albeit a human one. He is right too that he has little cause to seek Duncan's death other than ambition, which his own imagery configures as an excessive, wild and dangerous force. Considering Macbeth's inability to have children, something we will come on to discuss a little later, the personification of pity as a 'new-born babe / Striding the blast', as if riding into battle against him, and of 'Heaven's cherubin', riding like an angel army upon the air, suggest his as yet subconscious and deepest-lying fears of Banquo and his offspring.

In Macbeth's second soliloquy, his 'heat-oppressèd brain' appears to be working actively against him, conjuring an image of a bloody dagger hovering in the air. Shakespeare conveys Macbeth's horror at his own murderous intentions in a chain of images of evil - 'wicked dreams', 'witchcraft', 'Hecate' - to which he couples himself. Moreover, though he maintains a degree of separation through the distancing pronoun 'his', Macbeth imagines himself to be the figures of 'Murder', a rapist ['Tarquin'], and a ghost. The split in Macbeth's mind, born from his capacity to disassociate himself from his own actions, is evident here, a split that will widen into an abyss as the play progresses.

His third soliloquy in Act III Scene 1 conveys how soon after committing regicide Macbeth's regrets multiply and deepen. Although he has just about managed to patch himself together in public after his extreme agitation and distracted state immediately following Duncan's murder, the soliloquy confirms what the audience suspects - that only a thin tissue is covering Macbeth's mental torment. There are several sources of his anguish; most pressingly, he is not physically safe. He is afraid of Banquo, both of what he knows and of his friend's capabilities - his 'dauntless temper', 'wisdom' and 'valour'. Either loyalty to Duncan or personal ambition could drive Banquo to reveal Macbeth's treachery and/or to seek retribution. Moreover, reflecting on the Witches' prophesies, already too late in the day, Macbeth realises the full import of their claim that Banquo will be the 'father of a line of kings'. In a society in which fatherhood formed a vital cornerstone of male identity and was the bedrock of male power, Macbeth's sterility, his inability  to produce a son and heir, fundamentally undermines his authority and emasculates him. Hence his bitter references to a 'fruitless crown' and 'barren sceptre' and to the potent 'seeds of Banquo'.

And the cost to Macbeth of killing the 'gracious' Duncan, seizing the crown with an 'unlineal hand' and placing it in the hands of Banquo's 'issue'? The loss of a far greater, far more precious prize than this hollow, temporary trinket, his 'eternal jewel', his soul, to the devil. Although he determines to try to fight against 'Fate' and is jolted out of his anguished thoughts by the arrival of the murderers, the full force of this realisation opens up a void, an essential emptiness, in Macbeth that will hollow him out and fatally undermine him through the rest of the play.

This sense of existential emptiness finds its fullest and bleakest expression in Macbeth's final soliloquy, in Act V Scene 5. [In Aristolean terms, this is Macbeth's anagnorisis, his moment of piercing self-revelation, the moment where the fogs lift and he sees everything clearly for the first time.] Informed of his wife's suicide, Macbeth can only respond with numb indifference. His world-weariness and sense of emptiness has become all-consuming. His thoughts are nihilistic: Nothing matters, nothing lasts; life is a bleak comedy, death only a matter of time. His image of our lives being like those of actors recalls the 'all the world's a stage' speech from *As You Like It* as well as many other similar images in Shakespeare's plays. In some senses, this revelation shows Macbeth is still astute and perceptive; unlike the naïve Duncan, he completely understands how behaviour in public is always a kind of acting, and how this has been so much more acutely the case for him. But, in Macbeth's configuration of this metaphor there is no private half, no real, underlying self, to be revealed when the actor takes off his costumes and wipes off his make-up. Accordingly, Macbeth's metaphors emphasise insubstantiality – a 'brief candle' easily blown out by the wind and a mere 'walking shadow' without any corporeal body.

And, yet there is a grandeur in how poetically he expresses himself and there is comfort too, for him, in his words. If nothing matters, then it does not matter that he has committed atrocities, or that he will soon die. Conveniently, God and eternal punishment and the imagery of heaven and hell are noticeably far from Macbeth's mind. But he can take only scant comfort, perhaps. Macbeth's final soliloquy may close with a self-serving attempt to deny the consequences of his actions, but simultaneously it exposes the all-encompassing emptiness at the core of his being.

Critical essays on characters

There are dangers in providing exemplar essays. Inadvertently, such exemplars can close down the space for your own thinking and encourage uncritical regurgitation of an essay's content in examinations. Our essays were not written in timed, examination conditions and they are not examples of what an examination board would expect from any student in those conditions. Hence, primarily, our essays are not designed as model answers. Moreover, fundamentally, we don't believe there can be one model answer to literary questions. Furthermore, we believe the best essays express pupils' own critical thinking and opinions, supported by their teachers and informed by engagement with other readers. Hence our aim in the following essays is not to replace your own thinking, but rather to provoke, stimulate and inform your ideas about the play's major characters and to make you reflect more critically on their roles and functions.

Hopefully, our essays will make you think again, perhaps even make you think differently. Sometimes you may also encounter readings with which you disagree. Good; so long as you can explain and justify why you have come to different conclusions. Whether you mostly agree with their interpretations or not, these essays should, however, provide plenty of information you can digest, ponder, alter, reformulate and contest in your own critical voice.

Remember when you are writing about characters to try to lift your perspective above the character-level action of who said what and who did what to the author-level perspective of why these words and actions are significant.

Macbeth

As Laurie Maguire points out, 'Shakespearian tragedy often concerns individuals miscast in the part they are required to play... Macbeth, who murders for a living and loses no sleep over it, finds that killing a king causes nightmares.'[22] But, surely, as a fearsome and courageous soldier Macbeth is perfectly cast as a king within a militaristic feudal world where warrior virtues are not only valorised but are essential to the survival not only of individuals but also of nations. Look at how vulnerable Scotland was under the rule of saintly, but weak Duncan. Surely, by the terms of the world of the play, at least in the opening acts, Macbeth is a heroic character, forged by his times.

On the other hand, in the last speech of the play Malcolm passes a far sterner moral judgement on the Macbeths, labelling Macbeth a 'dead butcher' and his wife a 'fiend-like' queen. Of course, it suits Malcolm's propagandist purposes to present the Macbeths simply as embodiments of evil, setting up, as it does, a stark, black and white contrast with how he will supposedly rule. To some extent, though, Malcolm is surely right: Macbeth butchers the innocent Duncan and then proceeds to rule Scotland as a bloody tyrant, imposing his will on others through fear and ruthless brutality, ordering the murder of women and children and anyone who stands in his way, including his own friend, Banquo. He ends the play alone in his castle with a character unsubtly called Seyton, ordering his own men to be hanged if they show fear. By the end Macbeth has surely become a vicious, pitiless butcher, a monstrous 'hell-hound' or 'hell-kite', as Macduff calls him.

---

[22] Maguire, *Studying Shakespeare*, p. 129.

So which is he, Macbeth, a tragic hero or a villainous tyrant? Perhaps he starts the play as one but ends it as the other. Related to this question is to what extent Macbeth is a victim of his times or of supernatural forces or his wife or fate, and to what extent he must bear the responsibility for his increasingly bloody actions. These are questions with over which generations of critics have wrestled and on which we'll focus in this essay.

As an audience, can we entirely agree with Malcolm's simple judgement? We are likely, it seems, to feel uncomfortable with a description that is so sweeping and unambiguous. Calling Macbeth a 'butcher' suggests mindless, savage and indiscriminate violence. Is this an accurate description of his political assassinations of Duncan and Banquo? Of course, we follow Macbeth throughout the whole play, we are on the inside track of his kingship, have privileged, intimate access to his thoughts and insider knowledge about his relationship with his wife. We have, in short, been close-up to the fervent life of the Macbeths in a way we are never allowed to be with the rather cold-blooded Malcolm. Instinctively we may feel that Macbeth does, or at least did have, heroic qualities and that he is a more complex, less mindless character than Malcolm's biased and two-dimensional description allows.

What other arguments could we cite to contest Malcolm's reductive description of Macbeth as a 'butcher'? An obvious starting point would be whether Macbeth was entirely morally culpable for his actions. It could be argued that he had no intention of killing Duncan until first the Witches and then his wife intervened. Certainly, at the start of the play, Macbeth was a great hero, a warrior who has fiercely defended his King and his country from their bitterest enemies. However, when he happened upon the Witches, Macbeth became 'rapt' by their predictions. Perhaps, he was literally bewitched. Even so, in the face of his wife's demonically-driven insistence that he murder Duncan, Macbeth resolutely rejected the temptation, insisting 'we will proceed no further in this business'. In effect, Lady Macbeth only wins him over by blackmail and, if we read the imaginary dagger he sees in the air as he creeps towards Duncan's room as a projection of Lady Macbeth's hold over her husband, Macbeth may also be labouring under her demonic spell.

Moreover, even after the regicide, Macbeth shows he has not simply become a 'butcher'. Conscience, he implies, will not allow him to ever sleep again. He also fixates on the blood on his hands. While his wife is coldly practical and literal-minded, trying to reassure him that 'a little water clears us of this deed', her husband cannot even conceive of the possibility of cleaning so much guilt from his hand: 'Will all great Neptune's ocean wash this blood / clean from my hand? No, this my hand will rather / the multitudinous seas incarnadine'.

 Arguably these aspects of Macbeth's characterisation allow Shakespeare to keep the audience feeling at least some sympathy for him, despite his heinous crime. In addition, we may feel that Duncan was too weak a king and that his decision to make Malcolm his heir rather forced Macbeth's hand. We may even conceive of Duncan's murder as a political assassination made necessary by his manifold weaknesses as King, weaknesses that have made Scotland vulnerable to attack and fatally unstable.

Nevertheless, from the end of Act I onwards there's not much to keep the flame of sympathy for Macbeth flickering. Increasingly taking control of events from his wife, Macbeth also adopts her hellish idiom. For instance, in Act III Scene 2, like her, he calls up the forces of darkness to aid his plot to kill Banquo and Fleance: 'Come seeling night / scarf up the tender eye of pitiful day'. This is a fitting idiom for murders surely worse than the killing of Duncan: Banquo has been Macbeth's close comrade; Fleance is an entirely innocent child. Perhaps these murders are still not mindless butchery, but they are the actions of a ruthless political operator set on the path towards tyranny. After revisiting the Witches, on the basis that Macduff failed to attend his coronation Macbeth moves further down that path, vowing to 'surprise' the castle of Macduff and 'give to th' edge o' th' sword / his wife, his babe' and, indiscriminately, any 'unfortunate souls' connected to the household. Whereas, at a push, Banquo's murder could be deemed to have been politically unavoidable, Macbeth sends a brutal message via the Macduff murders to anyone who might stand against him. Indisputably, this is the behaviour of a tyrant and these are acts of brutal butchery. And from this point in the play onwards, it is not just Malcolm who calls Macbeth a monster, a butcher or a tyrant. As his rule runs its bloody course, many other characters express similar horror. Even those who had been loyal to him, such as Lennox, switch sides. By the time Lady Macbeth's suicide is reported to him, Macbeth is so numbed by butchery that he feels nothing. He has 'supped' so 'full with horrors' that he has become almost inhuman, little more than the monster or devil that his enemies label him.

Macbeth is a play of doubles and double-dealing. Several characters, double with Macbeth and provide telling contrasts – Duncan, Banquo, Malcolm, Macduff. Shakespeare's depiction of the English King, Edward the Confessor, also serves to reflect and emphasise Macbeth's descent into tyranny and monstrosity: Whereas Macbeth is increasingly associated with hell, Edward is religious, saintly and pious; whereas Macbeth embodies the sickness at the heart of Scotland, Edward cures his subjects by his saintly touch. Whereas Macbeth's motivation is driven entirely by selfish impulses, Edward is selfless; whereas nobody fights on Macbeth's side accept mercenaries, Edward is able to raise a powerful army, and so on.

The evidence that Macbeth becomes both a tyrant and a butcher is overwhelming. And yet many critics have argued that the audience, nevertheless, retain sympathy for Macbeth, despite his bloody actions. Why? Maybe the fact that Edward remains an off-stage and hence rather abstract character makes it hard for us to really identify with him. Maybe we also have unanswered concerns about Banquo, Malcolm and Macduff. Maybe we retain some sympathy for Macbeth, because unlike Banquo, he is not and cannot be a father, a fact that both fatally undermines his regal authority and torments him with the idea he has sacrificed everything, even his soul, for a hollow, 'fruitless' crown. Maybe we even admire Macbeth's willingness to fight to the very last and to defy fate. Our critical judgement might be softened a little by the fact that he shows some remorse for killing Macduff's family. It also seems likely that modern audiences, and critics, will be less inclined to forgive Macbeth's political murders than audiences and critics formed in harsher, more violent times. On the other hand, Jacobeans may well have viewed Macbeth's murder of Duncan as going against the will and authority of God. Hence readings of Macbeth's character change over time. In addition, our response to dramatic characters may also not be defined entirely by moral concerns. Macbeth is the most dynamic, powerful and vivid character in the play and an audience may be swayed, even entranced by his dramatic charisma.

The long-dominant, traditional method of interpreting Shakespeare's tragedies also encourages us to retain some sympathy for Macbeth. Under the influence of the philosopher Aristotle, for generations critics have read Shakespeare's tragedies fundamentally as stories of great men brought down by a weak spot, a tragic flaw, called in Aristolean terms, a 'hamartia'. This kind of reading interprets Macbeth as an essentially brave, bold and noble man undone by one flaw in his character, his over-reaching ambition. Once his  ambition has prompted him to commit the first murder, all the others follow as consequences. Other critics have argued that Macbeth is fundamentally a victim, either of conflicting ideas of masculinity operating in the world of the play or of malign female supernatural agents, such as the Witches and his wife. The critic Sean McEvoy, for instance, sides with the first to these two readings, opining that Macbeth tries to straddle a schism in medieval values: In the play there is a 'cult of masculine military prowess among the nobles' that is in conflict with the 'value system by which the nobles claim to live', a value system which 'says that loyalty and faithfulness are what keeps the political order intact and functioning'.[23]

Neither the Aristolean-inspired or more modern approach is completely convincing, because, in different ways, they seem rather to excuse Macbeth responsibility for his own worst actions. But there is another, perhaps, more persuasive argument. Perhaps the audience maintains some degree of sympathy with Macbeth, despite everything he does, because he is able to

---

[23] McEvoy, *Shakespeare, the Basics*, p. 219.

express his own psychological suffering so acutely, almost as if it is happening to some else. Put another way, it is almost as if after the murder of Duncan that Macbeth's psyche fractures, so that he splits into two characters living inside one head, one half ordering and carrying out butchery, the other appalled by his own murderous behaviour. The latter Macbeth is like a sensitive, perceptive, tortured poet, expressing his mental anguish with unusually brilliant acuity. The self-reflective hyper-articulacy Shakespeare endows his protagonist with implies that, perhaps, in different circumstances Macbeth could have become a very different person.

Flick through almost any of Macbeth's later speeches, especially when he is talking in private and you'll find flashes of this most eloquent poet of mental anguish. We have already commented on Macbeth's immediate response after the murder of Duncan and his obsession with the blood on his hands. To this we could add phrases Shakespeare gives Macbeth, such as the horribly visceral 'O full of scorpions is my mind'. Perhaps the strongest example, though, is his response to his wife's death in Act V. Having reflected on his mental numbness ['I have almost forgot the taste of fears'] Macbeth expresses an overwhelming existential despair with magnificent bleakness:

'Tomorrow, and tomorrow, and tomorrow,
Creeps in this pretty pace from day to day
To the last syllable of recorded time;
And all our yesterdays have lighted fools
The way to dusty death. Out, out, brief candle!
Life's but a walking shadow, a poor player,
That struts and frets his hour upon the stage,
And then is heard no more. It is a tale
Told by an idiot, full of sound and fury,
Signifying nothing'.

The action of the play makes it clear that Macbeth becomes a tyrant and, yes as Malcolm claims, a butcher, and in some ways even a demon or monster. But, even despite our best intentions, it's hard for any audience not to respond to the human being Shakespeare repeatedly suggests is still hiding there somewhere underneath all the blood and gore.

Lady Macbeth

Shakespeare's portrayal of Lady Macbeth is a damning one. A monstrous parody of the typical Jacobean mother, wife and subject, at every turn Lady Macbeth fills the audience with horror at the depths of her depravity. We can almost hear the gasps of shock as she dares to utter her heretical ambitions, emasculates her husband and threatens the most violent of infanticides on her imagined child. Her eventual descent into madness and undignified off-stage death serve as dire warnings to any Jacobean woman who dared to challenge the patriarchy. In tandem with the subversive force of the Witches, Lady Macbeth embodies Jacobean fears of female power.

Lady Macbeth is introduced to the audience in Act I Scene 5 carrying a letter from Macbeth which she proceeds to read aloud. This opening soliloquy reveals her immediate thoughts and ideas, and they do not leave much to the imagination. The audience at this point may sympathise with Macbeth; a courageous and successful soldier, he has just won a fierce battle defending his king and country. The Witches interrupted his journey home to tell him he will be king – crucially, he did not seek them out. Whilst he 'burned with desire' to question them further, he was 'rapt in the wonder of it', suggesting that rather than fanning a passion already within him, the weird sisters sparked this flame.

This cuts to the very heart of the debate about Macbeth and the level of agency he has in carrying out regicide. Lady Macbeth's soliloquy can be used to support the argument that, without the intervention of the Witches and subsequently his wife, Macbeth is unlikely to have demonstrated the level of ambition required to subvert what conventional thinkers in a Jacobean audience would have seen as the 'natural order' or the 'chain of being'.

Lady Macbeth reacts excitedly to the news that Macbeth has been promoted, quickly digests this and moves on to the higher prize: 'Glamis thou art, and Cawdor, and shalt be what thou art promised'. The promotion is given merely a clause within her first sentence as she sweeps through the titles of past, present and future in a single breath. Her mind clearly races to the conclusion that Macbeth should bring about the premonition himself by killing Duncan, whilst it is reasonable to assume that Macbeth may consider the prophecy to relate to a potential future event. What follows is one of the most famous quotations in literature: 'thy nature, it is too full o'th'milk of human kindness'. Lady Macbeth is well aware that Macbeth lacks the killer instinct required to betray his king - the description is not a flattering one as it essentially feminises Macbeth with connotations of the lactating role of a mother. The milk symbolises both Macbeth's innocence and purity, but also his lack of masculinity in the eyes of his wife.

It is important at this stage to revisit Shakespeare's motivation in presenting regicide in this manner. Not only is a Jacobean audience receiving the message that this 'vaulting ambition' is an unappealing trait, but the regicide is attributed at this point primarily to women. The Witches who initially foretell that Macbeth will reach the highest rank of king do so in a manner which seduces and entrances him. Macbeth responds to this by admitting in an aside that gaining this rank would be a 'swelling act of imperial theme'. However, the idea of committing murder makes his 'seated heart' 'knock' at his 'ribs'. The thought of killing Duncan occurs to him very quickly upon hearing the news he is Thane of Cawdor, but just as quickly he dismisses it. He decides to leave his fortune to fate, stating to Banquo that 'chance may crown me,/Without my stir', and explaining his 'dull brain was wrought/ With things forgotten'. Little does he know that his fate is soon to be sealed through the letter he sends to his wife.

This letter arrives only briefly before Macbeth does, and as his imminent arrival is announced, Lady Macbeth's monstrous ambition is laid bare. Duncan's demise is perceived by Lady Macbeth as a forgone conclusion: the 'raven', a harbinger of death, announces his 'fatal' entrance.  A strong sense of foreboding is evoked by the unwitting Duncan making his entrance 'under' her 'battlements'. This foreshadows the 'double trust' the king is investing in the Macbeths - the battlements are there to keep enemies out and those inside safe, and there is a clear juxtaposition between the innocent faith he places in them and the evil plans of which he has no conception. Notice too that innocuous, but highly-significant pronoun, '*my* battlements'.

These murderous plans have obvious parallels with the gunpowder plot, as discussed elsewhere in this guide; but the linking of regicide to sin is not enough to satisfy Shakespeare's desire to flatter his monarch. The playwright has already delighted the audience and his king with the heinous portrait of the Witches, drawing on the ideologies which underpin James I's insidious tract *Daemonologie*. Now the two sins must form a nefarious marriage within the equivocation of Lady Macbeth. 'Come ye spirits' she commands, and her subsequent listing of imperatives creates an incantatory tone echoing the Witches. Every line firmly establishes her intent to subvert the natural order in what has now become a triad of sin: The natural order of the great chain of being is upended with her desire to kill the king; the natural order of the God-fearing Christian mortals is to be cast aside by the 'murdering ministers' of the living dead; the natural order of her gender is resisted as she implores the supernatural forces to 'unsex me here'. The inevitable weakness of her femininity is foreshadowed here as she strongly resists what is presented as the female capacity for 'remorse', the 'compunctious visitings of nature' and the nurturing capacities of her 'milk' which must be converted to 'gall' [poison]. She is not asking to be made into a man, rather she is asking for the weaknesses of her femininity to be stripped away. She succeeds in this for a time, more successfully than Macbeth, but her female weakness [as perceived by a Jacobean audience] is ultimately her downfall.

Once Macbeth and Duncan arrive, probably the most famous manipulations scene in literature takes place, as discussed elsewhere in this guide. Whilst Lady Macbeth is not present in Macbeth's subsequent dagger soliloquy, one interpretation of the dagger is that it is a metaphysical symbol of his emasculation. The manifestation of this ephemeral phallic image which lies tantalisingly beyond his grasp could symbolise Lady Macbeth's control of Macbeth, even when she is not present in the room. The influence of the supernatural is also clear, and Lady Macbeth's alignment with the Witches draws together the power subversive females have over Macbeth and lack of control he now holds over his own destiny.

The subversive acts of Lady Macbeth will not, of course, go unpunished. Whilst the audience may secretly delight in her flagrant abuse of the natural and social order as they watch the scenes unfold, it is paramount to Shakespeare's design that Lady Macbeth gets her comeuppance, and in the most undignified and terrifying of ways. After the murder of Duncan and once Macbeth has become king, increasingly he distances himself from his wife, excluding her from his plans. Frequently lost in his own thoughts and acting alone, Macbeth's language takes on his wife's demonic idiom. Meanwhile, increasingly marginalised and having gained so little from Duncan's murder, Lady Macbeth slowly crumbles into hysteria, before unceremoniously casting herself from the battlements she ruled over so dominantly at the start of the play. The calm and measured manner in which she initially responded to the murder of Duncan: 'a little water clears us of this deed', is brought back ironically to haunt her. In Act V Scene 1 she desperately tries to wipe from her hands the imagined blood and the stench of her crimes. But, in despair, she understands that, whatever she does, 'these hands' will 'ne'er be clean' [a none-too-subtle nod to the hand washing of Pontius Pilot as he absolves himself from the decision to crucify Jesus Christ]. Discovering that it is not so easy to escape moral responsibility, Lady Macbeth suffers the tortures of guilt and conscience.

Her fragmented, incoherent speech matches her fractured psyche as once again her language is filled with dark and sinister imagery. Rather than the incantation of the supernatural, this time Lady Macbeth's mind is filled with the inevitability of her damnation; 'Hell is murky!' and 'there's a knocking at the gate' - the latter paralleling the porter's speech which follows Duncan's murder. Juxtaposed to this is the language of the doctor and gentlewoman, whose religious imagery is of 'heaven' and those who have died 'holily' in their beds. They declare she needs the 'divine' as her moral sickness is beyond the reach of any physician. Their descriptions remind the audience of how we should align our own responses - Lady Macbeth has defied God and it is now down to Him to cast judgement upon her.

It is important in the middle of this speech that Lady Macbeth reminds us of the 'Thane of Fife' 'had a wife'. Her language here takes on an almost sing-song nursery rhyme rhythm which contracts with the incantatory tone of her introductory soliloquy. No longer a threatening figure, she has been reduced to a grotesque parody of her former self, muttering nursery rhymes rather than summoning 'murdering ministers'. She is referencing the dead, however, and she evokes the spirit of Macduff's wife who provides a convenient symbol of the Jacobean maternal figure, the idealised opposite to the subversive Lady Macbeth.

The blood she is unable to cleanse is not only of 'the old man' who had 'so much blood in him', but also of the woman who lost her life and the lives of her children as a direct result of the tyrannical path she set Macbeth upon.

Repeated questions throughout the speech once again provide a contrast with the self-assured imperatives which characterised her speech when we first met her. She has been driven mad by her inability to remain immune to remorse, and what she perceived as exclusively female 'compunctious visitings of nature' when she commanded the spirits to 'unsex' her. The vital message for a Jacobean audience is clear: the will of God and nature cannot be defied; order is restored when Lady Macbeth decides for herself to end her life. We do not witness this final act of violence as a mark of shame upon her character; she is not afforded the same dignity in death as, say Romeo and Juliet or Othello. Instead we hear about her death as it is reported to Macbeth by Seyton. Her husband's response is nihilistic; rather than being overcome with grief he is instead overcome by the pointlessness of life which he describes as 'a tale / told by an idiot, full of sound and fury / signifying nothing.'

What better way to condemn a character who has embodied all that King James I abhors? Underlining for us all that Lady Macbeth's life held no meaning, and that nothing she or her husband strove to achieve had any real significance.

Banquo & Fleance

Shakespeare seems to have intended Banquo to function as a mirror and foil to Macbeth, paralleling Macbeth's noble characteristics while using contrast to illuminate his flaws. In many respects, a case could be made for Banquo as the true hero of *Macbeth*. Like Macbeth, Banquo is a courageous warrior held in high esteem by the other characters. Like Macbeth, he receives prophecies from the Witches, but while Macbeth is corrupted by the promptings of his ambition and the goading of his wife, leading him to the heinous sin of regicide, Banquo recognises the Witches' evil intent and remains loyal to Duncan. Banquo also remains loyal to Macbeth, even after the murder of Duncan, whereas Macbeth cowardly orders his friend's assassination out of jealousy and paranoia. And while Macbeth remains childless, unable to establish a line of succession that was viewed by the Jacobeans as vital to the well-being and stability of the state, Banquo, through his son, Fleance, establishes a blood-line of kings that stretches down to James I, the contemporary monarch of Shakespeare's England and patron of the very play being performed. More than just a foil, in the words of the critic Coppelia Kahn, Banquo is 'Macbeth's ideal self-image'.[24]

Therefore, given Banquo's moral superiority over Macbeth, why is it that as an

---

[24] Kahn, *Man's Estate: Masculine Identity in Shakespeare* p.182.

audience we fail to emotionally respond to Banquo as the play's true hero? Partly, given the play's title and the high flights of poetry Shakespeare affords to its eponymous protagonist and his wife, we recognise the emotional and intellectual interest of the play lies with the Macbeths and their very human struggle with the destructive effects of power and ambition. In contrast, Banquo seems just a little one-dimensional. Partly, we might also question Banquo's motives and complicity in Macbeth's tyrannical rise to power given his own failure to tell anyone about the Witches' prophecies or act on his suspicions of Macbeth after Duncan's murder. But perhaps, most significant, is the impression Banquo's true importance does not lie in his actions, the depth of his characterisation or even in his relationship with Macbeth, but rather in the symbolic function he fulfils.

If we accept Kahn's argument that *Macbeth* is a play about the failure to achieve authentic masculinity, evidenced by Macbeth's dependence on his wife and the Witches, his rivalry with other men such as Banquo and Macduff, as well as his failure to produce children – particularly a male heir – we can see that Banquo is presented to us as Macbeth's antithetical counterpart, an idealised model of Jacobean masculinity. He is loyal to King and God and free from the influence of women [it is striking how many mothers and wives are effaced from so many so many of the parent-child relationships presented in the play such as Banquo and Fleance, Duncan and Malcolm/Donaldbain, Siward and Young Siward]. Most significantly, Banquo has produced a male heir; his position as father authenticates his male identity and rebukes Macbeth's 'fruitless crown'. In the play, as in Jacobean society, paternity upholds patriarchal order, with God ruling over the Earth, the King ruling over the nation and the father ruling over the family. However, masculine order is threatened by the destabilising influence of unnatural femininity within the play characterised by the Witches and Lady Macbeth. Given the chaos threatened to England by the failure of Queen Elizabeth to produce a male, it was essential that James I could be presented to the English as belonging to a legitimate line of succession, one he personally traced back to Banquo.

Both Macbeth and Queen Elizabeth were childless monarchs succeeded by the sons of the rivals they had executed – Banquo and Mary Queen of Scots respectively. In this context, we can see how Banquo functions not as the moral hero of the play, but as a deeply conservative symbol of the status quo and patriarchal order, upholding the legitimised kingship and the rule of the father deemed necessary for the health and well-being of the entire nation. Fleance, who speaks a mere two lines in the whole play, serves an equally integral symbolic function and is inseparable from Banquo as together they represent the necessity of patrilineal order to the legitimacy and functioning of the entire Jacobean society.

Shakespeare establishes Banquo's heroic credentials early in the play during the Captain's speech of Act I Scene 2, where, fighting alongside Macbeth, he repels the advancing Norwegian army and wins the victory for Duncan. The Captain's simile comparing both Macbeth and Banquo to 'eagles' and a 'lion' not only emphasises their fearless courage but also, through the heraldic  emblem of the lion, associates both warriors with regal status. While Macbeth's heroism is singled-out by the captain for his audacious defeat of the rebel Macdonald, Shakespeare also uses this account to suggest the character flaws that, while serving Macbeth well on the battlefield, contribute to his downfall in the political arena. For example, his habit of 'disdaining fortune' suggests an assertiveness and impatience that will lead to him taking the Witches' prophecies into his own hands by committing regicide rather than allowing fate to work its course and make him king, while his 'bloody execution' and brutal defilement of Macdonald's body foreshadows his violent descent into tyranny as well as his own death at the hands of Macduff. Shakespeare also links Macbeth to the 'rebel' Macdonald through the adjective 'worthy' used to describe both men, and to the traitor, the Thane of Cawdor', whose position Macbeth inherits. Banquo, by contrast, is free from such traitorous implications, although the description that both Macbeth and Banquo 'meant to bathe in reeking wounds or memorise another Golgotha', which alludes to the place where Christ was crucified, perhaps hints that Banquo shares some of the moral culpability for the killing of God's king, even if he is not actively involved.

The contrasts between Macbeth and Banquo become more pronounced in the succeeding scene, where they are both introduced to the audience and receive prophecies from the Witches. Both men are clearly interested in what the Witches have to say, but while the prophecy to Macbeth as one 'that shalt be king' causes him to lose his composure as he desperately pleads with the Witches to tell him more, Banquo, by contrast, remains aloof and cautious as one who 'neither beg nor fear your favours nor your hate'. Macbeth's disregarded command to the Witches to 'Speak, I charge you' renders him impotent and emasculated, whereas Banquo recognises the Witches' implicit threat to patriarchal order and traditional masculine authority that runs throughout the play when he observes how 'you should be women, / And yet your beards forbid me to interpret that you are so'. Banquo also appears immediately suspicious of Macbeth asking him 'why do you start, and seem to fear / Things that do sound so fair?', implying that not only has Macbeth harboured previous thoughts of dethroning Duncan, but also that Banquo has suspected such secret ambitions. Banquo's repetition of the adjective 'rapt' to describe Macbeth twice in this scene further points to an understanding of Macbeth as falling under the spell of the 'instruments of darkness' that reveal truths 'to win us to our harm', an insight into the Witches' equivocations that of which Macbeth remains fatefully ignorant, until it is too late. However, the greatest contrast between the two men lies in the nature of the prophecies they receive. While Macbeth is destined to be king, his childless state dooms his kingship to sterility and a failure to establish any dynastic line. In contrast, Banquo 'shalt get kings, though thou be none', leaving him 'lesser than Macbeth, and greater'. As the mythological founder of the House of Stuart that established an unbroken line of rule in Scotland from 1371 right down to the time of James 1, Banquo's paternality becomes his defining characteristic.

The issue of Banquo's responsibility in Duncan's death is an ambiguous one. It is in keeping with the overall tone of moral uncertainty and obfuscation that runs throughout the play from the Witches' opening declaration that ''Fair is foul and foul is fair'. Clearly Banquo was not involved in the plot to murder Duncan, nor had he any explicit knowledge of it. In Act II Scene 2, right before the regicide, Macbeth hints at his murderous intentions, telling Banquo 'If you shall cleave to my consent, when tis, / It shall make honour for you'. Intimating a future change of circumstance, Macbeth suggests that Banquo will be rewarded if he remains loyal to him. Banquo however, responds with the assertion to 'keep / My bosom franchised and allegiance clear', making it clear to Macbeth that he will not go along with anything that threatens his conscience or loyalty to Duncan. Following the discovery of Duncan's body, Banquo once again reiterates his allegiance to God and the King, declaring how 'In the great hand of God' he will 'stand and thence' fight against 'treasonous malice'. Banquo upholds the Divine Right of Kings, the idea that God appoints his chosen king to rule in his name, a notion championed by in his book *Basilikon Doran*. Why is it then that Banquo fails to act on this pledge, despite having ample reasons to suspect Macbeth?

One possible explanation is that Banquo, despite his suspicions, passively allows the murder of Duncan to take place unchallenged, and refrains from acting against Macbeth after the murder because of the possible benefits to him promised by the Witches. In *Holinshed's Chronicles*, Shakespeare's original source for *Macbeth*, Banquo is portrayed as a guileful accomplice in Duncan's murder, and while Shakespeare no doubt altered Banquo's role and character to appease his patron, James I, something of Banquo's original moral complicity lingers on in the play. This is perhaps evident in Act I Scene 6, where Banquo and Duncan arrive together at Macbeth's castle. The scene is full of dramatic irony, with Duncan's description of the castle's 'pleasant' and 'sweetly' ambiance jarring with the audience's knowledge of how the Macbeth's are currently plotting to end his life. Macbeth's absence from the scene and failure to greet his distinguished guest further heightens the sense of foreboding. However, Banquo's reply to the king, describing how the

'temple-haunting martlet' makes its home in the masonry of the castle, while intended to confirm Duncan's positive impression of the castle, is so excessive in its imagery, that we suspect Banquo is seeking to convince himself as much as Duncan of the castle's benign environment, and that, on a deeper, perhaps subconscious level, Banquo is aware of the threat to Duncan's life. As Nicolas Tredell argues, Banquo's speech to Duncan 'can be seen as softening Duncan up, allaying a suspicion of Macbeth that Banquo himself feels'.[25]

On this reading, Banquo's choice of words such as 'haunting', 'heaven's breath' and 'delicate' take on more negative and sinister connotations, with 'delicate' implying Duncan's fragile hold on power and life, and 'haunting' and 'heaven's breath' suggesting his proximity to death. Furthermore, the martlet can be seen as a metaphor for Banquo himself, making his home among the cold and intimidating order of Macbeth's tyrannical rule in the same way the martlet makes its home among the 'jutty, frieze, buttress' of Macbeth's militaristic abode. The martlet's 'procreant cradle' and ability to 'breed' among the barren and sterile structure of the castle also highlights the central antithesis between Macbeth's childless state and Banquo's role as father, which not only leads to Banquo's death but also his return to 'haunt' Macbeth's empty 'temple'.

Banquo's moral complicity, or at least, ambiguity, is evident elsewhere in the play. His passing of his sword to Fleance at the start of Act III, while praying to 'merciful powers' to 'restrain in me the cursed thoughts that nature gives way to in repose' as well as his admission he has been dreaming of the Witches, imply Banquo may have been harbouring thoughts of dispatching Duncan himself, although crucially, unlike Macbeth, he does not act on them. Banquo's brief soliloquy after the coronation of Macbeth as King also implies how, rather than fighting against 'treasonous malice' as he had vowed to do after Duncan's murder, Banquo has made his peace with Macbeth's reign, despite his suspicions that he has 'play'dst moust foully for it'. His hope to equally gain from the Witches' prophecies explains Banquo's laissez-faire approach to Macbeth's rule. His final words, 'But hush! No more', indicate his intention to keep his suspicions about Macbeth to himself in the hope of becoming 'the root and father of many kings', a lack of action against Macbeth contributing to his complicity in Macbeth's tyrannical regime.

Within Act III Scene 1, Shakespeare parallels Banquo's soliloquy on Macbeth

---

[25] Tredell, *Macbeth*, p.97.

with Macbeth's succeeding soliloquy on Banquo, where he determines to have his friend killed by assassins. Macbeth reveals his jealousy of Banquo's noble characteristics of 'wisdom', 'valour' and 'royalty of nature', which no doubt would have flattered James I. Indeed, it is the potential to become a 'father to a line of kings' that Macbeth most fears, contrasting 'the seed of Banquo' with his own 'fruitless crown' and 'barren sceptre'. The imagery of sterility and infertility applied to Macbeth demonstrates how he is emasculated by the failure to produce sons and establish a line of descendants, in contrast to Banquo, for whose children Macbeth has committed regicide and now faces damnation. The conflict between Macbeth and Banquo therefore focuses around the issue of fatherhood and as Kahn argues, Banquo possesses 'a kind of greatness and power forever denied Macbeth – the power to procreate and specifically, have sons. Sexually and socially, in Shakespeare's world, fatherhood validates a man's identity'[26]. This is the true source of Macbeth's fear and jealousy that undermines his own sense of masculinity. In psychological terms, Macbeth projects these feelings onto the murderers he hires to kill Banquo by telling them how 'his issue' has held them 'under fortune' and 'beggared yours forever', subconsciously revealing his own male insecurities concerning Banquo and the usurpation of his throne by Banquo's descendants.

Even after death, Banquo continues to taunt and haunt Macbeth over his failed paternity. While the appearance of Banquo's ghost at Macbeth's coronation banquet [discussed in more detail in the Chapter on Act III in this book] has often been interpreted as manifesting Macbeth's subconscious guilt at the killing of his friend, Michael Hawkins has argued that in feudal societies like Macbeth's Scotland, banquets were symbolic of the host's power to control food supplies and provide provision for his subjects.[27] Banquo's appearance as a ghost and disruption of the banquet therefore calls Macbeth's ability as a fatherly provider into question. Lady Macbeth recognises the challenge Banquo poses to Macbeth's male authority and

---

[26] Kahn, *Man's Estate: Masculine Identity in Shakespeare* p. 183.

[27] Hawkins, *History, Politics and Macbeth*.

questions him 'What, quite unmanned in folly?' to which he responds if he could fight something that was alive he would not be 'trembling' like 'the baby of a girl'. Banquo's ghost therefore represents the haunting of Macbeth's failed masculinity.

Banquo's ghostly provocation sends Macbeth back to the corrupt and unnatural feminine influence of the Witches at the start of Act IV, but even here Macbeth cannot rid himself of Banquo's power and influence. While the third apparition of the crowned baby holding a tree in its hand is commonly interpreted as representing Malcolm and the approach of his army upon Dunsinane holding branches from Birnam Wood, it could also be read as representing a family tree that Macbeth lacks. The final vision the Witches show Macbeth is, of course, of Banquo's ghost, who, this time, reveals the line of eight kings that Macbeth fears will 'stretch out to th'crack of doom'. Powerless to stop Banquo's royal line and without any children of his own, Macbeth turns his impotent rage upon the destruction of Macduff's family, destroying his paternity instead.

It is the last we hear from Banquo. But, according to legend as recorded in *Holinshed's Chronicles*, his son, Fleance, fled to Wales where he married the

 Prince of Wales' daughter and fathered a son, Walter, who returned to Scotland to become steward to the king of Scotland. The title 'Steward' became 'Stewart' and after Walter married Robert the Bruce's daughter Marjorie, their son ascended to the throne in 1371 as Robert II, the first Stewart king. The House of Stewart ruled Scotland from this time until in 1603, the eighth king, James VI was crowned James I of England. Banquo's true significance in the play and source of power over Macbeth therefore lies not in Shakespeare's characterisation or his role in the plot, but rather in his symbolic function as a father, a father who not only upholds the Great Chain of Being that bestows paternal authority from God to King to Father, but also in his legitimizing of James' rule over Shakespeare's contemporaries. In this respect, Banquo truly is 'lesser than Macbeth, and greater'.

Macduff

After the Macbeths, Macduff is the next most important character in the play for two reasons: His strong narrative function as avenging anti-Macbeth and his symbolic representation of idealistic goodness. That said, he is dwarfed by Macbeth, as is every other character, in terms of stage presence. Whereas it is hard to escape Macbeth at any point in the play, Macduff is only sporadically present until Act V. In some cases, his conspicuous absence creates more impact than if he were present. His dialogues may be short, but they can be extremely powerful in content and imagery. Notwithstanding Macbeth, he is the most emotionally intense character in *Macbeth*, careening from horrified trauma to patriotic outrage to devastating grief and on to righteous fury. Despite his narrative subservience to Macbeth, ultimately, Macduff is a more successful and compelling character than either of Macbeth's major rivals, Banquo and Malcolm. Stepping into the role of furious avenger, it is Macduff who becomes Macbeth's nemesis, and Macduff who, with a sweep of his broad sword, delivers Scotland from tyranny.

His first appearance comes in Act I Scene 6 where he hovers in the background, a silent observer of Duncan's rewarding of Macbeth's patriotic valour. So what? Maybe is it no more significant than revealing how intimate he is with courtly norms and the political intrigue that is clearly strong in Scottish political life. Maybe it shows his intimacy with Duncan himself; Macduff appears to be one of the tried and trusted Thanes, a fact that would make his horrified outrage at Duncan's murder understandable. For it is here, in Act II Scene 3 that Macduff truly announces his arrival into the play, bringing with him huge energy and moral strength. Significant also is his role as the source of the incessant knocking that drums up so much  sonic tension in the preceding scene. Again, while not on-stage Macduff is still powerfully present, aggravating Macbeth's mental state. Critics have connected Macduff to a Medieval morality play called *The Harrowing of Hell*, which basically sees Christ beating on the door of Hell Castle demanding the release of trapped souls and this makes Macduff a Christlike saviour of a downtrodden people downtrodden people longing for liberating light. Certainly he makes a credible Christlike figure, battling and eventually defeating the evil tyrant 'butcher', enduring grief and ultimately restoring power to the God-appointed king, Malcolm, Prince of Cumberland. From the start, then, he is the epitome of the loyal subject and the noble man: he is 'the good Macduff'.

In Act II Scene 3, Macduff's horrified reaction is proportional to the transgression of Macbeth's regicide and his conversion of Duncan from good king to saintly martyr both idealises the dead king and amplifies the terrible taboo of Macbeth's murder. Macduff's language is hyperbolic and emotive, even claiming that language itself is inadequate to name the 'horror' he has seen: 'tongue nor heart cannot conceive nor name thee'. He also shows a commanding personality, rousing the sleeping caste with his resounding imperatives: 'approach the chamber'; 'Ring the alarum bell!'; 'Up, up and see'. In the midst of this great horror he also manages to show a chivalrous but deeply undeserved concern towards Lady Macbeth: 'O gentle lady, / 'Tis not for you to hear what I can speak'.

Shakespeare also subtly plants the seeds of Macbeth's distrust of Macduff. Firstly, Macduff publicly challenges Macbeth's decision to kill Duncan's attendants ['Wherefore did you so?'] and secondly, he and Banquo explicitly join to 'stand, and thence / Against the undivulged pretence fight / Of treasonous malice'. Macduff and Banquo are the main mechanisms of resistance against Macbeth in the play, but Macduff's dangerous public resistance is shown to be more effective that Banquo's silent misgivings. That said his resistance comes at a terrible price. Whereas Macduff is dynamic and effective in his organised resistance, Banquo is too hesitant and passive. Of the two Macduff is the man with the keener sense of morality and patriotism [Banquo, obviously, has a lot to gain by staying silent about his interactions with the Witches so his silence is understandable]. However, the political instability and treasonous uprisings that start the play have not made much impact on Macduff, as, while he may suspect foul play, he naïvely underestimates the depth of Macbeth's paranoia and the extent of his spy network. This naivety is highlighted when he decides to not attend Macbeth's coronation at Scone. Furthermore, and very dangerously, he refuses to attend Macbeth's celebratory banquet – one that begins Macbeth's reign not with the solidarity it should show but, instead, a public display of division, disloyalty and implications of illegitimacy. In this way, Macduff's idealistic morals are shown to be foolish and perhaps irresponsible. Ultimately, flawed and fatally limited in his political actions, he becomes a more complex, nuanced character than just a moral crusader.

Even more than the regicide, Macbeth's slaughter of the innocent Macduff family is his most amoral and appalling action in the play. Macduff represents no real threat to him in the context of the Witches' prophecies – that is Banquo and his issue. Shakespeare catalyses a turning away of the audience from Macbeth as this action suggests killing as no longer having any function but becoming an instinctive habit. The fact that Shakespeare allows the audience to see the touching, familial camaraderie between mother and son as well as their graphic murder on stage ensures moral disgust. However, our disgust is complicated by the fact that not only has Macbeth become a bloodthirsty 'butcher' but Macduff's patriotism has left his innocent family vulnerable to attack. His wife  is under no illusions about this as she complains bitterly to Ross about Macduff's abandoning of them: 'his flight was madness'. Even more damning, she suggests a foolish perhaps even callous, prioritising of country over family: 'He loves us not; / He wants the natural touch'. Notably, in this male-dominated warrior world, this voice of criticism is female and may be easily dismissed. However, Ross' defence of Macduff as 'noble, wise, judicious, and best knows / The fits o' th' season' rings particularly hollow. Macduff's actions simple do not bear this out. While his family's murder provides the motivation for Macduff's noble avenger role in the play, it also reveals a foolishness that is damning of his character, suggesting a blind idealism that could be manipulated.

This weakness is further highlighted by Malcolm in Edward the Confessor's court, where a worrying suggestion forms that Macduff might be similarly manipulated by Malcolm when he is king. Act IV Scene 3 allows the audience to witness Macduff's desperation to restore Scotland to Duncan's type of benign rule. So desperate is he that he is prepared to compromise his moral character to facilitate Malcolm's return as king. It is an excruciating scene from Macduff's perspective, with Malcolm's testing pushing him to the limits of moral compromise. Curiously, but understandably, Macduff is prepared to accommodate Malcolm's pretended lechery ['we have willing dames enough'] and avarice ['Scotland hath foisons to fill up your will / of your mere own'], showing a willingness to compromise to get what he wants. However, he will only bend his moral boundaries so far: Impressively he declares Malcolm 'Fit to live? / No, not to live'. While prepared to accept some degree of noble ignobility [not a great advertisement for rulers in general] he cannot accept a complete degenerate. It is an explosive statement in an age that believes in the divine right of kings, and it endows Macduff with a transgressive potential as great as Macbeth's. While Macbeth commits actual regicide, Macduff perpetrates a symbolic regicide by deposing the tyrannous Macbeth from the throne, thereby shielding the new king Malcolm by ensuring he is not tainted by this act. The crucial difference between Macduff and Macbeth is that while the latter operates for personal advancement, the former seeks for patriotic harmony. Hence his achievement of personal and political vengeance feels so satisfying.

However, this does lead to an interesting interpretation of Macduff and Macbeth as being, essentially, two sides of one coin! In Freudian terms, Macduff is the ego to Macbeth's id[28]: One is drawn to the light-filled piety of Edward's court, the other to the dark dynamism of the Witches; one doggedly personifies a type of social conscience, while the other is driven by primal impulses and wildest desires [once he rejects the constraints of conscience].

---

[28] According to Sigmund Freud, the mind is divided into three parts which he labelled the superego, ego and id. The superego contains the internalised rules of our culture shaping our morality, the ego is essentially our rationality, while the id contains our most basic, animalistic fears and drives.

Such an interpretation proposes the two men as doubles, or doppelgangers, and they are worryingly similar: Both are warriors who defeat usurpers and gruesomely decapitate them; both are outwitted by deceiving superiors smarter than them; both have nothing to live for by the end of the play; both are intensely dynamic, yet active in their own downfalls; both make risky decisions that backfire spectacularly; both are single-minded pursuers of their goals [but are driven by different objectives - individual gain vs patriotic stability]. But, despite these similarities, the poignancy of Macduff's raw grief at the slaughter of his family reveals a humanity that Macbeth's numbed reaction to his wife's suicide does not. Ultimately, Macduff is an essentially good, but flawed man. Shakespeare avoids presenting us with a simple personification of absolute goodness, which given the many striking similarities with Macbeth, is typical of a play where absolutes are constantly confused and denied, where 'fair is foul and foul is fair'.

The Witches

Among the most iconic and enduring of characters in all literature, the 'weird sisters' are firmly embedded within our cultural consciousness. Their incantatory 'hubble, bubble, toil and trouble' immediately conjures fearful images of withered hags chanting spells over a boiling cauldron. Whilst we now playfully dress up our children as witches on Halloween, or hold fancy dress parties and invite our friends to arrive as scantily-clad members of the occult, it is important to cast aside the healthy scepticism of the modern age and take ourselves back to the Jacobean era where to portray yourself as a witch would have been a very dangerous game indeed.

The word 'witch' has its etymological roots in Old English [wicce]. Prior to the Christianisation of Britain between the seventh and eighth centuries witchcraft formed part of the Anglo-Saxon paganism which existed in the part of Britain we now know as England. The subsequent Viking invasions in the ninth century eventually brought with it 'heathen' settlers and the belief in witchcraft was suppressed in the ninth and tenth centuries, following the *Laws of Ælfred* [ca. 890] and Christian authorities. However, a blending of pagan ritual and Christian practices had taken place during this period, and there is still evidence of Britain's pagan roots today. Christmas, for example, is celebrated at the time of the winter solstice and Easter can be traced back to Eostre, or Eostrae, the goddess of springtime and fertility. In addition, pagan places of worship were not destroyed. Instead they were converted into Christian churches. Christian belief in saints and miracles parallel pagan belief in gods and goddesses and the power they have to carry out supernatural acts. By the sixteenth century English Christians retained a fearful reverence for the supernatural and the power they believed could be harnessed for both good and evil. Macduff and Malcom discuss this topic when gathering their forces in England, marvelling at Edward the Confessor and his 'miraculous' and magical healing powers. Malcolm witnesses these acts and believes that Edward 'solicits heaven' in order to cure those suffering from 'ulcerous' disease. Once again, the play echoes contemporary history: James I had revived the so called 'royal-touch' alongside his re-establishment of the Divine Right of Kings. According to James I, not only were kings appointed by God, they could also perform miracles by utilising their God-given powers.

It is important, therefore, to appreciate that the supernatural does not purely exist in the form of evil within the play. The English armies could be interpreted as godly crusaders; sanctified by their King, they fight to re-establish Christian purity against the transgressive, hell-bound court of Macbeth, a court repeatedly referred to using the extended metaphor of disease and corruption. Macduff also could be seen as a saint-like figure, one who has sacrificed his entire family to oppose the hellish Macbeth. More than this, Macduff is imbued with supernatural qualities of his own; he appears twice in the visions of the Witches: Macbeth is told to 'beware Macduff' and, conversely, he is told 'no man that's born of woman' can have power over him. The fact that Macduff is later established to have been 'untimely ripped' from his mother's womb reveals him to have been part of the Witches' deadly trick. He is fated to carry out his anointed role, from birth it seems, and, given the rarity of caesarean sections in the eleventh century, there is a miraculous quality to the manner in which he was delivered alive from his mother's corpse. Divine forces presided that day, implying that Macduff was born to carry out the fatal attack on Macbeth.

The struggle between good and evil portrayed by Shakespeare in *Macbeth* could be viewed as mirroring the struggle that James I portrayed in his own writing. James' tract *Daemonology* had identified the threat the king believed Britain faced from supernatural evil. This threat of evil is juxtaposed with the divinity James believed he was imbued with as a divinely appointed representative of God on earth. Cleverly Shakespeare aligns James I with Edward the Confessor and the English king's miraculous healing qualities as well as with the incorruptible Banquo whose 'seed' goes forth to produce the line of kings from whom James I is prophesied to descend. In contrast to this are the wicked witches who, along with Macbeth's bewitching wife, corrupt 'brave Macbeth' until he becomes a tyrant.

The eleventh century setting for *Macbeth* was useful to Shakespeare. It allowed him to play with the wild historical imaginings of a Jacobean audience whose pagan ancestry was now more than half a century behind them. The suppression of witchcraft had taken place approximately a hundred to two hundred years before *Macbeth* is set, so the witches are introduced as living outside of society in 'a desert place'.

The Witches arrive on stage in the midst of a storm, and some historians have suggested that fireworks were set off on the Globe stage to announce their arrival. The threatening explosions and accompanying thunderous sound effects would have been likely to shock and awe the audience in a dramatic opening few moments. The trio of witches offer a sinister inversion of the holy trinity; we are entering the parallel realm of the supernatural, a realm in which everything heavenly has its hellish double. In pagan Britain storms had been moments of great supernatural power when the gods asserted their presence. Given the open-air daytime performances at the Globe, the Witches' entrance in the stormy gloom would have had to be conjured by the power of Shakespeare's language. The playwright had to employ every literary tool at his disposal to generate electrifying tension. One of the most obvious tools is the rhythm and metre of the Witches' speech. Whilst most Shakespearean blank verse is written in iambic pentameter, wherein the stress is placed on the second syllable in a foot, the Witches speak in trochaic tetrameter where the stress is placed on the first syllable in the foot: '**When** shall **we** three **meet** a-**gain**' in contrast to 'So **foul** and **fair** a **day** I **have** not **seen**' - the first words uttered by Macbeth in the play [which, in terms of imagery, hints at the hold the Witches already have on him]. Inversion of the naturalistic iamb symbolises the 'unnatural' qualities of the Witches. The trochees also help to create the

Witches' rhythmic chant-like speech, reinforced by the rhyming couplet. The second witch also uses a rhyming couplet. But the third witch converts this to a triplet: 'done' and 'won' neatly chimes with 'sun'. Supernatural manifestations of evil they may be, but the Witches' speech is concise and business-like. There is no sense of uncertainty regarding their plans. They will meet again and the meeting will take place when the 'hurlyburly' or battle has ended. Hence there is a sense of inevitability about Macbeth's fate; it has been sealed even before the Witches cast their spells. Their closing 'fair is foul and foul is fair', chanted by all three at once, upsets the nature order and is, as we have noted, uncannily echoed in Macbeth's speech when he enters in Scene 3.

The Witches' speech is also characterised by their repeated references to trouble-making and ill will towards seemingly law-abiding members of the

community. A sailor's wife who refuses to share her chestnuts is cursed via her husband; the first Witch declares she will sail to him in a 'sieve', an impossible task for mere mortals, and the other witches eagerly support her by supplying wind for her journey. The poor sailor can then expect to 'dwindle, peak and pine' for 'sev'nnights nine times nine'. His journey will be extended to eighty-one nights, and she goes on to explain that, spitefully, she would like to sink the ship altogether if she can. This little aside is important because it appears to nod towards the sources of the animosity James I felt towards witches. James had blamed witches for the difficulties his fiancée's ship had faced in reaching England. The king believed that the storm his fiancée had encountered had been deliberately created by witches. This vindictive behaviour, described in such detail, is made all the more galling for the audience as it was a woman who angered the witch in the first place, bringing trouble and strife on her husband through no fault of his own. Does this foreshadow Macbeth's own fate? A man, going about his business drawn into the malevolent and mysterious ways of spiteful women and suffering the consequences?

With this in mind, it is useful to compare this first meeting of the Witches and Macbeth with the second one in Act IV Scene I. Once again we meet the Witches before Macbeth, this time in a cavern with a boiling cauldron in the middle. Clearly they are living on the outmost margins of society, living like primitives or animals. Significantly, Macbeth chooses to seek them out on this occasion. Whilst their first meeting feels accidental to Macbeth as he returns home across the heath, the second time Macbeth chooses to visit the Witches, demonstrating how far he has sunk into depravity as he consciously consorts with these devilish creatures. The Witches are aware of his impending arrival and are preparing for it as the audience joins them in what has probably become one of the most iconic scenes in theatrical history. The trochaic tetrameter characterising the distinctive and unnatural speech of the Witches is adopted as they cast their spell and the audience gain a frightening insight into their worst imaginings of these supernatural beings.

'Thrice the brinded cat hath mew'd' the first witch announces, immediately adding to the tension of the bubbling cauldron with her incantatory rhythm and tone. For Jacobeans witches were real - the diabolical agents of a devil who could trick the unwary into the endless torments of hell. It is difficult to underestimate the level of fear that might have been engendered in the hearts of a Jacobean audience at this point. Indeed Shakespeare had been warned against using real spells such as these live on stage, but he went ahead anyway.

Notoriously a series of unfortunate incidents followed the staging of the play which has led to actors even to this day superstitiously believing it to be cursed. The title *Macbeth* is not to be uttered inside a theatre staging the play, rather it is referred to as 'The Scottish Play'. Legend has it that the actor playing Lady Macbeth died suddenly, leaving Shakespeare himself to take on the role and that real daggers were switched with fake ones leading to the onstage death of the actor playing Duncan. And to this day, many actresses when uttering Lady Macbeth's invitation to 'spirits' to 'unsex her' and fill her full of 'direst cruelty' like to wear a crucifix, just in case her summoning spell might still work.

Given the terrifying content of the Witches' spells, it is unsurprising these legends arose. This initial reference to a 'brinded cat' is likely to have been a reference to the devil, who took the form of cats and other creatures known as witches' familiars. 'Greymalkin' and 'Paddock', who are later referred to, have been described as animals the Witches utilise to invocate the devil's presence. The fact the cat mews 'thrice' is significant, drawing on the magical quality of the triad. Again, it appears that unseen, higher powers, beyond those of Macbeth and the Witches are really responsible for these events. This meeting is fated to happen now, in this place, as communicated via this particular cat which is set apart from all others. The 'brind[ing]' literally just means striped or patterned, but this is the <u>brinded</u> cat, which implies the markings carry particular devilish significance. The Witches' spell goes on to incorporate ingredients which were not only horrifying, such as 'finger of a birth-strangled babe', but also exotic, frightening and intoxicating, such as a 'tiger's chaudron'. Travel to the lands of this fearsome creature was rare for Jacobeans; clearly the reach of the Witches' power is extensive enough for them to get hold of a tiger's entrails and, moreover, the scales of a dragon.

The arrival of Hecate, the tri-formed goddess of witchcraft, is the source of much controversy. Many Shakespeare scholars believe she did not appear in the original play, but her addition some time later reflects a growing campaign

against witches in Jacobean England. Placing an even more powerful witch within the scene creates a sense of hierarchy. A greater sense of urgency is therefore needed to tackle an organised and powerful threat to society. Hecate's appearance is brief and her primary purpose is to chastise the Witches for their lack of consultation with her in dealing with Macbeth. The scene reinforces the orchestrated nature of Macbeth's manipulation; when he arrives he is quite literally walking into a carefully laid trap and everything he sees is designed to coerce him. The vision of the disembodied armoured head which advises him to 'Beware Macduff' and the subsequent visions of children are devised to push him towards the killing of Macduff's children. Each prophecy fools him into believing that he is still in control of his own destiny: Macduff is a mere mortal who can be defeated; the second apparition assures him that none of 'woman born' can harm him. Of course, the visions must come in threes. The third again is posed as a riddle: 'Macbeth shall never vanquished be until / Great Birnam Wood to high Dunsinane Hill / Shall come against him'. There is something infinitely satisfying for an audience about a puzzle such as this - we all know the tragic arc must end in Macbeth's downfall, so how might this seemingly impossible event take place? The dramatic irony adds fuel to the simmering tensions of the scene, particularly when Macbeth arrogantly states 'That will never happen'.

Whilst each of these apparitions have been designed to quell Macbeth's fears and further inflate his hubris, his final burning question demonstrates that underneath it all, Macbeth knows the truth of the Witches' prophecy to Banquo at the start of the play – that Banquo's heirs will become kings. The line of eight kings accompanied by Banquo's ghost confirm this to him, and once again Shakespeare's nods to king James I's pure and incorruptible lineage as a descendent of Banquo. It is no accident that the audience are reminded of Banquo's purity and innocence at this point in the play, and indirectly of their first meeting. The prophecy provided could have sparked equal ambition within Banquo; he could have attempted political manoeuvres to ensure his son Fleance was positioned to eventually gain the throne. Instead Banquo leaves his fate to higher powers: 'In the hand of God I stand' is his position. As James I believed himself to be the earthly 'hand of God', the message of the play seems clear - place your fate within the hands of your king and you will be rewarded. Despite all of the forces against Macbeth, ultimately he was open to their corruption. 'Look how my partner's rapt' Banquo comments as he witnesses the influence the Witches exert upon him. Equally, he has the opportunity to step from his regicidal path as he soliloquises upon the nature of his 'vaulting ambition'; 'we shall go no further in this business' he declares to his wife. Once again, he is seduced by her manipulations and is firmly set back on the path to his downfall. Witnessing this, the audience is encouraged to reserve its most damning judgements not for the hideous Witches, who, after all show no power to directly impact on the play's action, nor for the calculating Lady Macbeth, but for the corruptible man who should have known better than to listen to them.

Of course, the Witches embody Jacobean fears of supernatural evil. In addition, they are the embodiments of contemporary male fears about powerful women. The Witches are 'wild', i.e. ungoverned by social norms, including gender norms, 'withered', i.e. unfertile and unmaternal, and also 'bearded', like men. Lady-like women, such as Lady Macduff, are not a source of fear; it is women who reject their femininity and take on masculine traits that really terrify the male Jacobean psyche. And, whereas Lady Macbeth's motivation for her 'unsexing' herself was to aid her husband's quest to become king, what really drives the Witches' pervasive malevolence remains an unresolved and disturbing mystery.

Other characters

Prematurely levelled by Macbeth's unnatural and sinful regicide, the benign king Duncan is not only a catalyst for Macbeth's spiral into amorality but also forms an essential part of Shakespeare's meditation on the theme of kingship. Four kings are present in *Macbeth* and each one of them offers some insight into the nature of political rulers: Duncan, Macbeth, Edward the Confessor

 and Malcolm. Duncan and 'the most pious' Edward are explicitly connected to each other through descriptions of their religious piety. Macduff describes Duncan as 'a most sainted king' and upon discovering his corpse in Inverness castle compares the regicide to the sacrilegious ransacking of a temple: 'Most sacrilegious murder hath broke ope / The Lord's anointed temple'. Even Macbeth describes Duncan's corpse in the language of precious metals [language that calls to mind portraits of saintly martyrs in religious art]: 'his silver skin laced with his golden blood'. Admittedly, Macbeth utters this trying to deflect his killing of Duncan's two attendants, but his words draw upon a wider view of Duncan as a devotedly pious king.

There is a slight, but maybe crucial, difference between Duncan and Edward's reign. Edward is a holy healer and rewards his people with spiritual health and the promise of future stability ['tis spoken, / To the succeeding royalty he leaves / The healing benediction'] whereas Duncan rewards with materialistic gifts of status. Macbeth, for instance, is given an additional title and Lady Macbeth is given a 'diamond'. In stark contrast to Duncan, who fails to interpret the present, let alone the future, Edward also 'hath a heavenly gift of prophecy'. Duncan's gullibility and naïve trusting of others is shown as a fatal weakness. He complains bitterly about the original Thane of Cawdor's treachery: 'He was a gentleman on whom I built / An absolute trust', and then replaces this traitor with Macbeth. Naïvely Duncan takes at face value what he sees and hears and is blind and deaf to disguise and duplicity. His lack of mental acuity and sophistication is cruelly apparent in his misinterpreting of Inverness castle as a 'pleasant seat' where 'the air / Nimbly and sweetly recommends itself', whereas the audience knows it is a place of despicable treachery and murderous intent. Shakespeare's use of dramatic irony ensures that Duncan appears fatally innocent and even foolish.

The intensity of Macduff's reaction to Duncan's murder may reflect the status of Duncan within the play as a good king. But is he a good king in another fundamental sense, i.e. is he good at being a king; is he a successful king? The evidence suggests not. Despite his saintly ways and the intense loyalty he evokes in men like Macduff, his kingdom is a shambles of social upheaval, teetering on the brink of collapse. The first act establishes a Scotland on the brink of social implosion, threatened by both internal division [Macdonald and Cawdor] as well as external invasion [the Norwegian Sweno]. Additionally, the fact that Macbeth can, and clearly has in the past, envisioned regicide as a stepping stone to individual advancement is worrying. Lennox and Ross too are worryingly ambiguous in their political loyalties, which implies that though Duncan may be saintly, he's not a compelling leader. That said, Shakespeare implies that Duncan's rule may be weak and leave his country vulnerable, but it is better than Macbeth's vicious tyranny.

In contrast, Shakespeare presents Duncan's son, **Malcolm**, as a much more functional, pragmatic alternative to his father. Where Duncan was gullible and gushing in his praise of the violent men who served him, Malcolm is a far shrewder man, despite his unworldly inexperience of kingship and the battlefield. Like his brother, **Donalbain**, Malcolm is quick to realise appearances can be deceptive. In their brief, anxious exchange after their father's death, for instance, Malcolm comments that showing 'unfelt sorrow' is something the 'false man' does easily, while his brother comments perceptively that 'Where we are / There's daggers in men's smiles'.

Malcolm may lack the warrior prestige that Macbeth possesses, but he seems quite able to command men like Macduff and Old Siward for his own purposes. Notable is Shakespeare's refusal to show Malcolm in combat, so we have no idea of his aptitude for violent conflict, the expertise that made

Macbeth a most 'noble' and 'worthy gentleman' in Duncan's eyes. His liberating forces are characterised not only by the rightness of their cause but by their youthfulness and it can be supposed that it is easier for Malcolm to inspire the 'many unrough youths' on his side rather than the more seasoned campaigners. In this way, Malcolm's inexperience becomes an advantage: He will have to create new ways of ruling after the catastrophes of the old ways [The weak kingship of Duncan and the tyranny of Macbeth]. Maybe he brings the most powerful attribute of them all: hope; hope for a better Scotland of the future where Thanes becomes earls and Scotland becomes more civilised, like its great neighbour, England.

So, if Malcolm lacks his father's saintliness and Macbeth's warrior brutality what does he bring? He seems to be a successful blending of Duncan's passivity and Macbeth's dynamism. His odd reaction to his father's murder ['O, by whom?'] may be perplexing from an emotional perspective, but it's shrewd from a political perspective. If he views himself as swimming with opportunistic sharks, his detached interest buys time to navigate the best escape from such dangerous waters. Rather than fall prey to his 'strong sorrow', he cleverly waits before decisively acting: 'I'll to England'. This skill of weighing up alternatives and being able to protect himself from treachery is most obvious in his testing of Macduff in England, where he has been gathering a liberating force, which itself shows grand ambitions.

Though impressive in its ingenuity, Malcolm's elaborate deceit is also worrying. While it may be a practical strategy for self-preservation, it's hardly the stuff of inspiring leaders: 'modest wisdom plucks me / From over-credulous haste'. It is also notable that Shakespeare uses Malcolm to articulate the perfect king bucket list: 'justice, verity, temperance, stableness, / Bounty, perseverance, mercy, lowliness, devotion, patience, courage, fortitude'. While he refutes his own defaming lies, his claims to be the opposite of what he pretended to be are not immediately convincing. Macduff's measured response: 'such welcome and unwelcome things at once / 'Tis hard to reconcile' suggests he has not been entirely won over. Like Macduff, the audience will want to see these kingly virtues enacted rather than claimed. Again, while unquestionably a more effective leader than his father, Malcolm certainly doesn't possess the inspirational nature of Edward, who is presented as the ideal king; a devout, religious man who can also use military force wisely. To be fair to Malcolm, his liberating expedition to Scotland is successful and his level-headed, clear command is impressive. Significantly and, perhaps astutely, by allowing Macduff his vengeance on Macbeth, Malcolm avoids committing the heinous sin of regicide. Disappointingly, his bland victory speech ['What's more to do / Which would be planted newly with the time'] has worrying echoes of Duncan's claims to 'plant thee, and will labour / To make thee full of growing,' suggesting a possible return to familiar cycles of unstable rule. At the margins of the play lurks Fleance and the rest of Banquo's lineage, who must forcefully wrench the royal throne from Malcolm's [or his descendants'] grip. Hence the celebration of Malcolm restoring the natural order upon a fractured state and heralding a new bright future, a New Scotland if you like, always seems a little unconvincing.

While **Lennox and Ross** are no more that minor figures, they allow directors to indicate the experience of living under both Duncan and Macbeth. Often appearing together in scenes, especially early in the play, both enter with Macbeth after he kills Duncan's two attendants. Was this a chance for Macbeth to bribe them for their loyalty or might they be actual accomplices in the murder of the attendants? Lennox was certainly there, attesting that 'their hands and faces were all badged with blood'. Some productions use Lennox and Ross to illustrate the treachery of the Scottish court by having Lennox become 3rd Murderer when Banquo is killed. A notable 1971 film version even showed Ross leaving the Fife castle gates open for the murderers of the Macduff family, who are his kin.

In a general sense, Ross seems no more than a mouthpiece who delivers generous dollops of exposition around the play. It is he who relays how Macbeth vanquished Sweno and the almost disastrous foreign invasion; it is he who tells Macbeth he is now the new Thane of Cawdor; it is he who has the conversation with the old man about the unnatural nature of the regicide; it is he who tells Macduff about the slaughter of his family; it is he who tells

Old Siward about his son's death in battle. It is notable that Malcolm, a good, reliable reader of men's characters refers to Ross as 'the worthy Thane of Ross' and he is not seen doing anything morally reprehensible in the play. Indeed, while Lennox stays put in Scotland, Ross journeys to England to meet Macduff and Malcolm. As a 'cousin' of Macduff he is essentially kin to goodness.

Given his role of serving the narrative rather than being a complex character, Ross is often shown as a political functionary of the various regimes, keeping his head down and, perhaps, really serving only his own best interests. In the terrible scene where the Macduffs are slaughtered, he 'dare not speak much further'. Significant too is the fact that he doesn't do anything useful to protect his vulnerable cousins but, instead, worries about making a show of himself: 'should I stay longer, / It would be my disgrace and your discomfort.' Lady Macduff would probably choose discomfort over death, though! This expedient passivity could also be seen at the play's end where he tells Old Siward about his son's brave death in combat. Given the ease of victory, one could assume that Ross has not played any significant role in the fighting; he may have observed it, but unlike Macbeth and Macduff, he is not a fighter.

While Ross seems to have a distinctly expositional function, Lennox appears to be just around a lot, but saying very little: He is a silent witness in Duncan's court; he accompanies Macduff to wake Duncan; he goes with Macbeth to inspect the murder scene; he accompanies Macbeth to see the Witches, once again is a silent witness, this time of Malcolm's taking of the throne. However, there are some suggestions that while Ross does a lot of talking, Lennox does a lot of listening as a court spy. Macbeth boasts of a spy network that allows him to monitor the Thanes: 'There's not a one of them but in his house / I keep a servant fee'd'. Tellingly, it is Lennox who brings Macbeth word that Macduff has fled to England and, even more interestingly, in Act V he claims to 'have a file / Of all the gentry' who form part of Malcolm's liberating forces. Lennox is the Thane closest to Macbeth and addresses him as 'Ay my good lord,' which, of course, could be necessary flattery rather than sincere allegiance.

The fact that he can appear as Macbeth's loyal servant in Act IV Scene 1 and his next appearance in Act V sees him proclaim that they need to do 'so much as it needs / To dew the sovereign flower, and drown the weeds' shows a well-informed political opportunist, one willing to do what is required to survive in a violent, unstable state. Essentially Shakespeare portrays Lennox as an informer whose morality is flexible and dubious [hence why he is sometimes seen taking on the role of 3rd Murderer and enthusiastically bringing news of Macduff's flight]. A short scene that confirms his fickle, self-serving allegiances is Act III Scene 6 where he seems to be engaging in an odd double-speak with an anonymous Lord. In fact, it is from this conversation that Lennox gleans the intelligence that Macduff has fled, but Lennox manages to seem to both praise Macbeth ['Was not that nobly done?'] and criticise him [describing Scotland as 'our suffering country / Under a hand accursed']. The ambiguity of his conversation has led to interpretations of his behaviour as either the insidious gathering of intelligence from Macbeth or the necessary double speak needed to survive in the midst of violent tyranny. Wherever Lennox's true loyalties lay and whatever his motivation may have been, crucially, at some point between Acts IV and V he switches allegiances and joins the victorious side.

Critical reception

We haven't the time or space here to go into a lot of detail about how different critics, readers, audiences and theatre practitioners have responded to the play since it was produced over four hundred years ago. And, while different perceptions of the play are certainly interesting and can help us see our own responses in a clearer light, they are not required at GCSE and, indeed, only have to be lighted touched upon even at A-level. It is useful to form some sense, however, of how the general focus of criticism of this play and Shakespeare's plays as a whole, has changed over time.

Broadly speaking, though it is a highly varied field, traditional critical approaches have tended to be preoccupied with issues concerning the principle characters. As we mentioned in our section on the nature of the play, Aristotle has had, and continues to have, a huge influence on literary criticism, particularly criticism of tragedies. Aristotle's description of the central protagonist as being a high-born character who destroys himself because of a tragic or fatal flaw in his character or via a calamitous decision he makes has encouraged critics to focus on the titular characters of Shakespeare's tragedies. Examining Macbeth, Lear, Hamlet and Othello critics suggested a range of different possible 'hamartias' for each of these tragic heroes.

One very influential critic has been A.C. Bradley. In the book of his lectures, *Shakespearian Tragedy*, first published in 1904 and still in print, Bradley focuses mainly on the major characters in each tragedy, exploring what he takes to be their individual psychologies as a means of discovering their true hamartias. Bradley expresses 'awe' at the character of Macbeth and claims that within the fearsome warrior lurks 'the imagination of a poet'. For Bradley, Macbeth's fatal flaw is his over-reaching ambition.

Generally Bradley treated Shakespeare's characters as if they were really living, breathing people and even speculated about their lives beyond the world of the plays. Beginning after World War II Modern criticism seeks to correct the traditional over-focus on major characters by re-directing our critical attention on to the wider contexts which shape character and characterization, particularly history, society, politics and power.

Modern criticism is highly sceptical about the idea that human beings operate in the world entirely as free agents, making all our own choices and decisions without influence from our culture or society. Modern critics point out that just as a text is shaped by the time it was written in and the time in which it is read, so too are the characters within it. In a nutshell, these critics relocate the hamartia in Shakespeare's plays from the protagonists to the societies and the times in which the plays are set. At the same time, modern critics often dispute the traditional idea that mysterious, supernatural or heavenly forces control the worlds of Shakespeare's plays. Dealing with *Macbeth*, such critics are likely to interrogate the idea that the Witches control events, arguing instead that they merely predict, or even just prompt the human characters into making things happen.

A typical modern critical approach might also examine how Macbeth is destroyed not by faults within his own psyche but by unresolved and contradictory forces within his society. As we referenced in our essay on the play's protagonist, Sean McEvoy, for instance, argues that in the 'feudal Scotland of Macbeth violence is the means by which power is achieved and held; but the value system by which the nobles claim to live says that loyalty and faithfulness are what keeps the political order intact and functioning'[29]. In other words, there is a deep ambivalence about violence in the play and an invisible seeming line between sanctioned murder and non-sanctioned murder, a line over which Macbeth fatefully steps.

Other critics, taking a similar tack to McEvoy, argue that Macbeth is destroyed by irreconcilable notions of manliness, while others suggest the fundamental flaw in the world of the play is the over investiture of power in the figure of the king and the lack of counter-balancing forces within society. Meanwhile

---

[29] McEvoy, *Shakespeare the Basics*, p.219.

critics such as Coppelia Khan focus on the significance of fatherhood in the construction of male identity and masculine power.

As Robert N. Watson puts it in his essay, *Tragedies of revenge and ambition*, 'The changes in Shakespeare's world, like the Witches in *Macbeth*, generated a foggy, confusing moral landscape, and then destroyed people for not finding the same old path through them.'[30]

---

[30] Mceachern [ed.], *The Cambridge Companion to Shakespearian Tragedy*, p.178.

Teaching & revision ideas

Whichever board's exams you'll be taking, a fundamental part of the test will your knowledge of the play. Check this by trying to write out a summary of the play, scene by scene, without using the script. Try to write no more than a couple of sentences for any one scene. Once you're done, compare your summary to our one.

How many scenes are there in the play overall? Twenty-nine, which is quite a lot. *Hamlet*, for instance, only has twenty. Work out how many there are in each act and then check against our tally, on the last page of this book.

Now try to write out the narrative of the play in continuous prose using only about one side of A4.

In the following example we have summarized the play, scene by scene for you. Unfortunately for you some witch has cast a spell on the summary, overturning its natural order. Your task is to be the healing goodness that restores the correct order. Only once you've had a thorough stab at this task are you allowed to check against our version at the back of the book.

- The Witches meet and chant their spell.
- An old man and Ross discuss the unnatural murder and the darkness that has 'strangled' the morning light. Macduff confirms that suspicion for the murder has fallen on the fleeing sons and that Macbeth will soon be crowned the new king.
- The murder of Macduff's son and wife.
- Macbeth and Banquo bump into the Witches on a heath who prophesy Macbeth will become Thane of Cawdor and then King. Their prophesies are less favourable for Banquo.
- In his castle, still defiant, with only the aptly named Seyton for company, Macbeth learns that his wife has died. Makes his great, despairing, nihilistic speech about life being a 'tale told by an idiot… signifying nothing'.
- A very short scene, building up to the battle. Malcolm orchestrating

the assault on Dunsinane.

- Macbeth fights with and kills Young Siward. Enter Macduff. It seems the castle has been easily taken as 'the tyrant's people on both sides to fight'.
- The banquet. Macbeth hosts a celebratory banquet, but his attempts to radiate magisterial calm are upset by the timely entrances of Banquo's ghost. Lady Macbeth frantically tries to cover for her husband's wild abstractions.
- Lady Macbeth receives a letter from her husband outlining recent events, worries over his too-kindly nature and resolves to fortify him. In the second of her soliloquies in this scene she calls up evil spirits to 'unsex' her and turn her into a witch. When Macbeth enters his thoughts are in his face and she tells him he must look 'like the innocent flower/ But be the serpent under't'.
- Lady Macbeth sleepwalking scene. No longer can things be covered up.
- The aftermath of battle. Enter Macduff with Macbeth's head. Malcolm has the final say about ridding Scotland of 'this dead butcher, and his fiend-like queen'. Final celebratory flourish of trumpets.
- Duncan orders the traitor Cawdor to be executed, greets Macbeth as his 'most worthy cousin' and announces that his son, Malcolm will succeed him as King of Scotland.
- Duncan and his entourage hear reports of Macbeth's defeat of the rebel Macdonwald and of the invading Norwegians.
- Macbeth returns to his wife after committing the assassination. Unable to pray, in a highly-agitated, guilt-ridden state, he has forgotten to leave the daggers at the scene of the crime to frame Duncan's guards. Infuriated, Lady Macbeth takes the daggers to do what her husband failed to do.
- A porter jokes about guarding 'hell-gate'. Lennox reports that there has been great disorder in nature during the night. Macduff discovers the murder of Duncan. Macbeth apologies for killing Duncan's guards in his 'fury'. When Macduff questions this Lady Macbeth faints. Banquo expresses 'fears and scruples' and promises to fight against the 'undivulged pretence'. Everyone leaves except Duncan's sons,

Malcolm and Donalbain. Understanding that 'there's daggers in men's smiles' they decide to flee, to England and Ireland respectively.

- Banquo fears that Macbeth has 'playedst most foully' in becoming king. Meanwhile, in his third soliloquy, Macbeth is feeling insecure and worried about Banquo: 'Our fears in Banquo/ Stick deep'. Macbeth convinces some desperate men to kill Banquo for him.

- Power hasn't brought happiness to Lady Macbeth either. She is also fretting; 'nought's had, all's spent' and a distance has grown between her and her husband. He tells him to remain 'innocent' of his plans for Banquo and says that his 'mind is full of scorpions'. Whereas earlier in the play it was Lady Macbeth who was plotting murders and evoking evil spirits, now it is Macbeth.

- The murder of Banquo, and Fleance's escape.

- The goddess of witchcraft, Hecate, upbraids the Witches.

- Lennox confides his fears to anonymous Lord, referring openly to Macbeth as a 'tyrant', a word the lord also uses. We hear that Malcolm is safely stowed at the court of the 'most pious' English king, Edward the Confessor.

- Macbeth and Macduff fight to the death. Surprisingly Macbeth expresses remorse: 'my soul is too much charged/ with blood of thine already'.

- Banquo is troubled by what he has witnessed and exchanges ambiguous words with Macbeth about his loyalty. Macbeth lies to his friend about not thinking of the Witches. In his second soliloquy as he moves through the castle towards Duncan's bedchamber, Macbeth hallucinates, seeing a 'dagger' floating in the air before him.

- Desperate to learn the worst, accompanied by Lennox, Macbeth visits the Witches. They conjure apparitions which make ambiguous prophecies about Macbeth's future. In his fourth soliloquy Macbeth decides to 'surprise' Macduff's castle and slaughter all who are found therein.

- In England Macduff is trying to persuade Malcolm to return to Scotland and fight for the throne. Malcolm tests Macduff's loyalty by pretending to have a series of vices that will make 'black Macbeth' seem 'as white as snow'. Malcolm lists the kingly virtues and a doctor reports King Edward's miraculous healing powers. News arrives of the death of Lady Macduff and her children. Malcolm's forces are ready.

- Enter with 'drums and colours' Malcolm's army. A host of new minor characters, along with Lennox, who last time we saw him was by Macbeth's side.
- In a room within the castle in his first soliloquy Macbeth changes his mind and resolves not to kill Duncan. His wife greets this decision with scorn and hatches a plan of how to carry out the murder. Cowed, Macbeth agrees to murder his king.
- Macbeth expresses disdain for the 'boy' Malcolm and says he will 'fight, till from my bones my flesh be hacked'. He asks the doctor whether there is any cure for a 'mind diseased'. The doctor makes a sharp exit.
- Duncan arrives outside Macbeth's castle of Dunsinane and is greeted by the gracious-seeming Lady Macbeth.
- In the woods of Birnam soldiers are hacking down branches to cover their numbers, hence fulfilling the Witches' prophecy.

The minor, secondary characters can all-too-easily slip under the radar of our critical attention. Tracking them, however, can often be a useful and incisive way of re-reading the text, one that can open up new perspectives. Albeit always rather out of the spot-light of dramatic attention and in the background, Lennox and Ross appear in many scenes. Check exactly in which scenes they appear and what they say. What would be lost if these two characters were cut from the play?

Our understanding of principle characters is constructed from what they say and do and through their interactions with other characters. Write down a list of all the characters in the play, including minor and unnamed ones. Now think about what the interactions with each of these characters reveals about Macbeth. For instance, although we never see the Captain on stage with Macbeth it is clear from Act I Scene 2 that the former admires the latter and sees him as a fierce and brave warrior. Once you've considered all the interactions with Macbeth switch to another major character and repeat.

Using the list above track all the different roles taken on by the major characters. For Macbeth, for instance, we might start with general in the Scottish army, apparently loyal servant of the King, friend to Banquo, beloved husband and so forth. Which characters play multiple roles and which ones are most consistent?

Lady Macduff and her son only appear in one scene. Imagine a director wished to cut this scene but an actor strongly disagreed. If can work in pairs, take a part each, prepare you arguments and conduct a short debate. Is this scene really necessary? If so, what does it contribute to the drama?

Re-read our analytical commentary for Act I Scene 7. Although in all productions Lady Macbeth must persuade her husband, the tone and manner the actress chooses can vary widely. We've read the scene as Lady Macbeth's belligerence cowering her husband into changing his mind. Experiment with other ways to play the scene. Could, for instance, Lady Macbeth speak more gently than we've imagined? Then watch at least two different versions of the scene. One of these versions should be brilliant McKellen/ Dench one:
https://www.youtube.com/watch?v=blkL-2UQkXo
Compare the different versions, focusing on the actors' movements and tones. How do they vary from each other and from our analysis?

Write the names of all the major characters on separate pieces of paper. Turn the paper over, face down and mix together in a pile. Working with another student, randomly pick three pieces of paper at a time. For your three characters decide which two go best together and which one of three is different and separate. Try the different ways of pairing the characters and decide on the strongest one. Put the pieces of paper back into the pile. Mix and pick again. Continue while the exercise remains interesting and productive.

Using a piece of A4 paper, draw a series of four concentric circles. In the middle circle write down how any one of the major characters sees themselves or any insight we have into their private thoughts. In the second inner circle write down how the character interacts with other major characters, e.g. friend, enemy, confidante. In the next circle write down how other characters think of the major character. In the last circle write down your own thoughts about the character. In the remaining space around your circles add any other opinions about the characters you come across in lessons or from films or wider reading.

[Our last exercise is for teachers, but could be adapted if you're a student working with some friends.] Roll an intellectual hand grenade into the classroom with a controversial opinion about the play. For example, 'Lady Macbeth is a victim of a vicious patriarchal world and deserves our sympathy' or 'Macbeth is no more than a plaything for malevolent supernatural forces and can only be pitied'.

Students work in groups of four, two opposing pairs with Pair A agreeing with the statement, Pair B disagreeing.

1) They have three minutes to formulate their points with extra points for use of convincing textual knowledge - one student writes, the other presents.
2) Then it's two minutes each to present their case with the opposing team noting relevant points. Pair A goes first, then Pair B.
3) Each pair then has a minute to formulate any relevant rebuttal points. Next Pair B has thirty seconds to present their rebuttals, followed by the same from Pair A.
4) Finally, the pairs reveal their inner Lennoxian treachery and switch sides, i.e. Pair B arguing for and Pair A arguing against the critical opinion. At this stage you can consider splitting the groups so each pair takes on a new pair. Or if the argument is reaching fever pitch the groups can stay as is. This time though the pairs switch writing and presenting duties.
5) Once the debates have run their course, the pairs collate their findings.

6) Students now work individually to reflect upon their findings and can add further points/modify existing points/sourcing more/better textual evidence. Ultimately, they must take a side, but may change their initial starting position if they want.

The end product is a discursive essay that conveniently argues the proposition they've been working on in class.

GLOSSARY

ALIENATION EFFECT – coined by German playwright, Berthold Brecht, it reverses the conventional idea that audience's suspend their disbelief when watching a play

ANTITHESIS – the use of balanced opposites, at sentence or text level

APOSTROPHE – a figure of speech addressing a person, object or idea

ASIDE – brief words spoken for only the audience to hear

CADENCE – the rise or fall of sounds in a line

CATHARSIS – a feeling of release an audience supposedly feels the end of a tragedy

CONCEIT – an extended metaphor

DRAMATIC IRONY – when the audience knows things the on-stage characters do not

FIGURATIVE LANGUAGE – language that is not literal, but employs figures of speech, such as metaphor, simile and personification

FOURTH WALL – the term for the invisible wall between the audience and the actors on the stage

GOTHIC – a style of literature characterised by psychological horror, dark deeds and uncanny events

HAMARTIA – a tragic or fatal flaw in the protagonist of a tragedy that contributes significantly to their downfall

HEROIC COUPLETS – pairs of rhymed lines in iambic pentameter

HYPERBOLE – extreme exaggeration

IAMBIC – a metrical pattern of a weak followed by a strong stress, ti-TUM, like a heart beat

IMAGERY – the umbrella term for description in poetry. Sensory imagery refers to descriptions that appeal to sight, sound and so forth; figurative imagery refers to the use of devices such as metaphor, simile and personification

JUXTAPOSITION – two things placed together to create a strong contrast

METAPHOR – an implicit comparison in which one thing is said to be another

METRE – the regular pattern organising sound and rhythm in a poem

MONOLOGUE – extended speech by a single character

MOTIF – a repeated image or pattern of language, often carrying thematic significance

ONOMATOPOEIA – bang, crash, wallop

PENTAMETER – a poetic line consisting of five beats

PERSONIFICATION – giving human characteristics to inanimate things

PLOSIVE – a type of alliteration using 'p' and 'b' sounds

ROMANTIC – a type of poetry characterised by a love of nature, by strong emotion and heightened tone

SIMILE – an explicit comparison of two different things

SOLILOQUY – a speech by a single character alone on stage revealing their innermost thoughts

STAGECRAFT – a term for all the stage devices used by a playwright, encompassing lighting, costume, music, directions and so forth

STICHOMYTHIA – quick, choppy exchanges of dialogue between characters

SUSPENSION OF DISBELIEF – the idea that the audience willing treats the events on stage as if they were real

SYMBOL – something that stands in for something else. Often a concrete representation of an idea.

SYNTAX – the word order in a sentence. doesn't Without sense English syntax make. Syntax is crucial to sense: For example, though it uses all the same words, 'the man eats the fish' is not the same as 'the fish eats the man'

TRAGEDY – a play that ends with the deaths of the main characters

UNITIES – A description of tragic structure by Aristotle that relates to three elements of time, place and action

WELL-MADE PLAY – a type of play that follows specific conventions so that its action looks and feels realistic.

Recommended reading

Bradshaw, G. [2012] *The Connell Guide to Shakespeare's Macbeth*. Connell Guides.

Brown, J. [ed.] [1982] *Focus on Macbeth*. Routledge.

Kahn, C. [1981] *Man's Estate: Masculine Identity in Shakespeare*. University of California Press.

Maguire, L. [2003] *Studying Shakespeare*. John Wiley & Sons.

McEachern, C. [2013] *The Cambridge Companion to Shakespearian Tragedy*. Cambridge University Press.

McEvoy, S. [2006] *Shakespeare the basics*. Routledge.

Palfrey, S. [2005] *Doing Shakespeare*. The Arden Shakespeare.

Siddall, S. [2002] *Cambridge Student Guide*. Cambridge University Press.

Smith, E. [2019] *This is Shakespeare*. Penguin.

Websites

The British Library, *Discovering Shakespeare: https://www.bl.uk/shakespeare*

Peripeteia.webs.com

The Royal Shakespeare Company: *Rsc.org.uk*

About the authors

Head of English and freelance writer, Neil Bowen has a master's degree in Literature & Education from Cambridge University and is a member of Ofqual's experts panel for English. He is the author of *The Art of Writing English Essays for GCSE*, co-author of *The Art of Writing English Essays for A-level and Beyond*, *The Art of Poetry* & *The Art of Drama* series. Neil runs the peripeteia project, bridging the gap between A-level and degree level English courses **www.peripeteia.webs.com,** and delivers talks at GCSE & A-level student conferences for The Training Partnership.

Neil Jones is an English teacher with a PhD in English Literature from Oxford University, where he specialised in modern poetry. Neil has contributed to two books in the *Art of Poetry* series.

An Irish English teacher, Michael Meally holds an MA in American Literature as well as first class degrees in English Literature and Engineering. Michael is the co-author of *The Art of Writing English Literature Essays* and has contributed to several of the *Art of Poetry* books.

Kathrine Mortimore is a Lead Practitioner at Torquay Academy. She has a master's degree in Advanced Subject Teaching from Cambridge University where she focused on tackling disadvantage in the English classroom, a topic she has continued to blog about at kathrinemortimore.wordpress.com. Kathrine has contributed to both the *Art of Poetry* and the *Art of Drama* series.

Act One has seven scenes; Act Two has four; Act Three has six; Act Four has three and Act Five has a whopping nine scenes.

Act One:

- The Witches meet and chant their spell.
- Duncan and his entourage hear reports of Macbeth's defeat of the rebel Macdonwald and of the invading Norwegians.
- Macbeth and Banquo bump into the Witches on a heath who prophesy Macbeth will become Thane of Cawdor and then King. Their prophesies are less favourable for Banquo.
- Duncan orders the traitor Cawdor to be executed, greets Macbeth as his 'most worthy cousin' and announces that his son, Malcolm will succeed him as King of Scotland.
- Lady Macbeth receives a letter from her husband outlining recent events, worries over his too-kindly nature and resolves to fortify him. In the second of her soliloquies in this scene she calls up evil spirits to 'unsex' her and turn her into a witch. When Macbeth enters his thoughts are in his face and she tells him he must look 'like the innocent flower/ But be the serpent under't'.
- Duncan arrives outside Macbeth's castle of Dunsinane and is greeted by the gracious-seeming Lady Macbeth.
- In a room within the castle in his first soliloquy Macbeth changes his mind and resolves not to kill Duncan. His wife greets this decision with scorn and hatches a plan of how to carry out the murder. Cowed, Macbeth agrees to murder his king.

Act Two:

i. Banquo is troubled by what he has witnessed and exchanges ambiguous words with Macbeth about his loyalty. Macbeth lies to his friend about not thinking of the Witches. In his second soliloquy as he moves through the castle towards Duncan's bedchamber, Macbeth hallucinates, seeing a 'dagger' floating in the air before him.

ii.   Macbeth returns to his wife after committing the assassination. Unable to pray, in a highly-agitated, guilt-ridden state, he has forgotten to leave the daggers at the scene of the crime to frame Duncan's guards. Infuriated, Lady Macbeth takes the daggers to do what her husband failed to do.

iii.   A porter jokes about guarding 'hell-gate'. Lennox reports that there has been great disorder in nature during the night. Macduff discovers the murder of Duncan. Macbeth apologies for killing Duncan's guards in his 'fury'. When Macduff questions this Lady Macbeth faints. Banquo expresses 'fears and scruples' and promises to fight against the 'undivulged pretence'. Everyone leaves except Duncan's sons, Malcolm and Donalbain. Understanding that 'there's daggers in men's smiles' they decide to flee, to England and Ireland respectively.

iv.   An old man and Ross discuss the unnatural murder and the darkness that has 'strangled' the morning light. Macduff confirms that suspicion for the murder has fallen on the fleeing sons and that Macbeth will soon be crowned the new king.

Act Three:

i.   Banquo fears that Macbeth has 'playedst most foully' in becoming king. Meanwhile, in his third soliloquy, Macbeth is feeling insecure and worried about Banquo: 'Our fears in Banquo/ Stick deep'. Macbeth convinces some desperate men to kill Banquo for him.

ii.   Power hasn't brought happiness to Lady Macbeth either. She is also fretting; 'nought's had, all's spent' and a distance has grown between her and her husband. He tells him to remain 'innocent' of his plans for Banquo and says that his 'mind is full of scorpions'. Whereas earlier in the play it was Lady Macbeth who was plotting murders and evoking evil spirits, now it is Macbeth.

iii.   The murder of Banquo, and Fleance's escape.

iv.   The banquet. Macbeth hosts a celebratory banquet, but his attempts to radiate magisterial calm are upset by the timely entrances of Banquo's ghost. Lady Macbeth frantically tries to cover for her husband's wild abstractions.

v.　　The goddess of witchcraft, Hecate, upbraids the Wtches.

vi.　　Lennox confides his fears to anonymous Lord, referring openly to Macbeth as a 'tyrant', a word the lord also uses. We hear that Malcolm is safely stowed at the court of the 'most pious' English king, Edward the Confessor.

Act Four:

i.　　Desperate to learn the worst, accompanied by Lennox, Macbeth visits the Witches. They conjure apparitions which make ambiguous prophecies about Macbeth's future. In his fourth soliloquy Macbeth decides to 'surprise' Macduff's castle and slaughter all who are found therein.

ii.　　The murder of Macduff's son and wife.

iii.　　In England Macduff is trying to persuade Malcolm to return to Scotland and fight for the throne. Malcolm tests Macduff's loyalty by pretending to have a series of vices that will make 'black Macbeth' seem 'as white as snow'. Malcolm lists the kingly virtues and a doctor reports King Edward's miraculous healing powers. News arrives of the death of Lady Macduff and her children. Malcolm's forces are ready.

Act Five:

i.　　Lady Macbeth sleepwalking scene. No longer can things be covered up.

ii.　　Enter with 'drums and colours' Malcolm's army. A host of new minor characters, along with Lennox, who last time we saw him was by Macbeth's side.

iii.　　Macbeth expresses disdain for the 'boy' Malcolm and says he will 'fight, till from my bones my flesh be hacked'. He asks the doctor whether there is any cure for a 'mind diseased'. The doctor makes a sharp exit.

iv.　　In the woods of Birnam soldiers are hacking down branches to cover their numbers, hence fulfilling the Witches' prophecy.

v.　　In his castle, still defiant, with only the aptly named Seyton for company, Macbeth learns that his wife has died. Makes his great, despairing, nihilistic speech about life being a 'tale told by an idiot... signifying nothing'.

vi.   A very short scene, building up to the battle. Malcolm orchestrating the assault on Dunsinane.

vii.   Macbeth fights with and kills Young Siward. Enter Macduff. It seems the castle has been easily taken as 'the tyrant's people on both sides to fight'.

viii.   Macbeth and Macduff fight to the death. Surprisingly Macbeth expresses remorse: 'my soul is too much charged/ with blood of thine already'.

ix.   The aftermath of battle. Enter Macduff with Macbeth's head. Malcolm has the final say about ridding Scotland of 'this dead butcher, and his fiend-like queen'. Final celebratory flourish of trumpets.

Printed in Great Britain
by Amazon